FABULOUS AT 50

FABULOUS 50

JANET MACCARO, PhD, CNC

SILOAM
A STRANG COMPANY

Most Strang Communications/Charisma House/Siloam/FrontLine/Realms products are available at special quantity discounts for bulk purchase for sales promotions, premiums, fund-raising, and educational needs. For details, write Strang Communications/Charisma House/Siloam/FrontLine/Realms, 600 Rinehart Road, Lake Mary, Florida 32746, or telephone (407) 333-0600.

Fabulous at 50 by Janet Maccaro, PhD, CNC
Published by Siloam
A Strang Company
600 Rinehart Road
Lake Mary, Florida 32746
www.siloam.com

All Scripture quotations are from the New King James Version of the Bible. Copyright © 1979, 1980, 1982 by Thomas Nelson, Inc., publishers. Used by permission.

Cover Designer: Judith McKittrick
Executive Design Director: Bill Johnson

International Standard Book Number: 978-1-59979-209-5

Previously published as *Midlife Meltdown* by Siloam, ISBN 1-59185-550-0, copyright © 2004.

07 08 09 10 11 — 9 8 7 6 5 4 3 2 1
Printed in the United States of America

Neither the publisher nor the author is engaged in rendering professional advice or services to the individual reader. The ideas, procedures, and suggestions in this book are not intended as a substitute for consulting with your physician. All matters regarding your health require medical supervision. Neither the author nor the publisher shall be liable or responsible for any loss or damage allegedly arising from any information or suggestion in this book.

The recipes in this book are to be followed exactly as written. The publisher is not responsible for your specific health or allergy needs that may require medical supervision. The publisher is not responsible for any adverse reactions to the recipes contained in this book.

While the author has made every effort to provide accurate telephone numbers and Internet addresses at the time of publication, neither the publisher nor the author assumes any responsibility for errors or for changes that occur after publication.

This book is dedicated to those of you who share the goal of living a long life with the ability to function at a high mental, physical, and spiritual level, and to those of you who seek an active and richly abundant life.

Contents

Age fifty is a pivotal point in life. This book is designed to help persons fifty and over manage every aspect of the midlife aging experience—dietary and health concerns, spiritual growth and maturity issues, anxiety and depression, the need to care for aging parents, and more. Each chapter will offer a protocol (a plan or method of action) to help spot, manage, and redefine the aging process—body, mind, and spirit.

This book is divided into two sections. In Part I, I redefine the aging process and talk about ways to zap the eight biggest age accelerators that you will be facing. I teach you how to fortify and strengthen yourself against these eight age-makers so that you can maintain or improve the level of health you currently have and boost it to the highest possible level. I also discuss stress, sleep, exercise, and the health of your soul and spirit.

In Part II, I outline each of the specific conditions commonly afflicting fifty-year-olds—everything from arthritis to skin health.

In these chapters I present antiaging/disease-preventing protocols consisting of supplement recommendations. There are many supplements you could take for each of these conditions, so to help you identify the best ones right away I have employed a two-tier system in these chapters. The top tier contains my "starred," or most highly recommended, supplements. These are the ones that have proven most effective and safe for that condition and are most strongly supported by clinical research. If you want even more help with that condition, begin trying the supplements in the second tier. These others may not have strong clinical support at this time, but they have a long track record of historical use for hundreds, if not thousands, of years.

Keep in mind that many times clinical studies are not performed on natural substances because of their lack of patent protection. A naturally occurring plant, vitamin, or mineral is not patentable (and therefore not profitable); hence the lack of clinical studies.

Do not be overwhelmed by the lists of recommended supplements. And don't take everything at once. Start with the protocol for anti-aging in chapter 2. Give it two to four weeks before adding anything else.

If you are battling a specific midlife condition, like adrenal exhaustion or stress, simply add to your protocol the starred supplement(s) outlined for that condition. Don't add more than two supplements at a time. Take the new supplement combination for two to four weeks before making a change. Assess whether or not you are getting the help you were hoping for. If after that time you still need more help with a condition, you may add items from the second tier for additional support. Again, don't add more than two new supplements at a time.

An effective antiaging program must deal with each individual's unique genetic, neuroendocrine, and biological systems. Putting together a youth-enhancing protocol is *not* one-size-fits-all. The following life-extending chapters will arm you with the best philosophies and therapies to make your fifties fabulous. In the following chapters, I will show you how to make fifty the new thirty by teaching you how to turn your hourglass upside-down.

Part I

MAKING FIFTY THE NEW THIRTY!

MAKING FIFTY
THE NEW THIRTY!

I have just celebrated my fiftieth birthday. I must say that as the days leading up to the event ticked by one by one, I had flashbacks of my grandmother, who at age fifty looked years older than her birth certificate declared. I remembered my mother and how she looked on my wedding day—she was fifty then. How much she had aged since my father left her, thrusting her into a life of pure survival and extreme responsibility, which quickly etched itself across her face.

Now…it's my turn. I've reached the half-century mark and am now an official card-carrying member of the AARP! Something I would tease my older friends about is now my reality.

I don't feel fifty. But I realize that while they say age is only a number, the fact that I *am* fifty means so many things in terms of my future state of health—body, mind, and spirit.

A dear friend recently sat down with me and pointed out something that illustrated the point very well. It made an impression upon me that will forever be stored in my amygdala. She simply drew the following:

Birth--------------------------X---------------Death

That summed it up. The X represents where I am at fifty. If I live to be eighty, then the illustration depicts how much life I have left.

This was a real wake-up call for me. With that in mind, I realized that millions of other baby boomers in this nation who are or who will be turning fifty need this book. This may be the most important body of work I have written because it will educate you on how to make fifty the new thirty. That's right!

It is possible. Our life expectancy has risen. It is now possible to live to be one hundred years old and beyond. If that is truly the case, then fifty really is the new thirty. Our parents and grandparents did not have access to all of the neutraceutical products that are at our disposal. They did not have the advances in all the healing and health-building modalities that we have.

You can make fifty the new thirty. You can be fifty and fabulous. My goal is to educate you on all the ways to extend your days and slow your aging process.

How can you turn back the clock and make your fifty feel like thirty in every respect?

First of all, you must realize that age fifty is a pivotal point in life. It is time to take a hard look at where you have been and where you want to go. You must analyze how you have spent the first half of your life. What mistakes did you make? What did you not do that your heart longed to do? Did you harbor unforgiveness? Did you love enough—and were you loved enough? Did you give all that you could? Did you sing, did you dance, and did you smell the roses along the way? Or did you spend the first fifty years of your life chasing wealth only to find that now you are chasing health?

To illustrate, I want to share with you the following from *Secrets of Longevity* by Dr. Maoshing Ni. The conversation between the Yellow Emperor, the first ruler of China, and his court physician took place over 4,700 years ago and it is relevant for all fifty-year-olds today:

"I have heard that in the days of old, everyone lived one hundred years without showing the usual signs of aging. In our time, however, people age prematurely, living only fifty years. Is this due to our environment or is it because people have lost the Way?" asked the Yellow Emperor.

Qibo, his court physician replied, "In the past, people practiced the Way. They understood the principle of...balance....They formulated practices such as meditation to help maintain harmony with the universe. They ate balanced diets at regular times, arose and retired at regular hours, avoided overburdening their bodies and minds, and refrained from overindulgences of all kinds. They maintained well-being in body and mind, thus it is not surprising that they lived over one hundred years.

"These days, people have changed their ways. They drink wine like water, indulge in excessive...behavior, drain their essence, and deplete their energy. Seeking emotional excitement and momentary pleasures, people disregard the natural rhythm and order of the universe. They fail to regulate their lifestyle and diet, they sleep improperly. They do not know the secrets of conserving their energy and vitality. So it is not surprising that they look old at fifty and die soon after."[1]

In today's world, many of us have also lost our "way," the way of achieving vibrancy through and beyond the age of fifty. But I believe that we can turn our realization of what we have been doing to undermine our vitality into a willingness to make the next "prime of life" just that! As the ninety-four-year-old, modern-day antiaging sage Art Linkletter states in his latest book, *How to Make the Rest of Your Life the Best of Your Life*, "Longevity is as much an act of will as a dedication to exercise and a healthy diet."

BODY, MIND, AND SPIRIT

Before you can begin to turn back your clock, you have to figure out what makes you tick. Did you spend the first half of your life as a survivor or as a victim? Survivors will find it easier to make fifty the new thirty because they have learned from the past and they use their hard-earned knowledge to propel them forward. They use the wisdom they have gained and the spiritual growth they have experienced as inspiration to continue on; faith and hope are their traveling companions, and they are ready to embrace the next half of life with enthusiasm. Victims, on the other hand, tend to be stuck at age fifty, paralyzed by the past, and unable to forgive and move forward. Even if you have been living in the victim role, the good news is that often, with this realization, healing can begin.

Completing the fifth decade of life can be an "aha" moment in which you celebrate and embrace with all that you have overcome and the milestones you have accomplished. Or, depending upon how you have spent your younger years, reaching the big 5-0 can be an "oh, no" moment.

If you have stressed too much, lived on too little sleep, eaten poorly, failed to exercise, and burned the proverbial candle at both ends, you will be left with a shortened wick at fifty. In other words, your bank account of physical, emotional, and spiritual health can be seriously overdrawn at midlife, which can lead to a midlife meltdown.

If you are a baby boomer, born between 1946 and 1964, this book is especially for you. Especially if you were born between 1957 and 1960, you have already or will soon reach fifty.

The past fifty years have been an explosion of innovation and new ideas. This generation has produced some of the best risk takers, problem solvers, and inventors ever. We have had freedom, failure, success, and responsibility, and we have learned how to deal with it all.

For women, fifty marks the end of their childbearing years, while for men it can mean andropause (male menopause), which becomes evident by increased irritability, decreased libido, and more. At this age, both sexes may begin to think about financial issues and retirement, although some people reach fifty with a positive, energized attitude that is anything but retiring.

Often age fifty brings with it internal stress and external pressure that becomes so intense that life offers little or no joy. Physical symptoms such as overwhelming fatigue and lethargy are often a constant battle, enthusiasm for things once cherished is diminished, hope is dashed, and uncertainty is plentiful. A freefall occurs as our "safety net" of invincible youth gives way.

Midlife meltdowns, as I call them, are occurring throughout this country as those of us fifty and older grapple with aging parents and children leaving home for college (only to return overqualified and unemployed). Marriages go through a myriad of changes, and divorce is more common than not. Poor lifestyle and dietary habits in the past have set the stage for inferior health conditions and degenerative diseases at midlife. The lack of a strong spiritual life becomes evident when you consider all the substance abuse or mood-elevating medications that are used by midlifers in attempts to cope with all the difficult midlife issues.

In other words, midlifers are stressed out, their bodies show signs of giving out, and many times they suffer from feeling left out and depressed as lifestyle changes occur, such as empty nests, divorces, and the need to care for aging parents. These stressors contribute to the body's breakdown—the physical aches and pains, and the emotional and spiritual depletion.

If you are fifty, you are probably experiencing many unsettling events in your life physically, relationally, emotionally, financially, hormonally, and more! I am approached by people from all walks of life who are fifty and older and who are aging faster than necessary in their bodies, minds, and spirits due to "sins of the past" coupled with the pressures of the present and the fear of the future.

HERE'S TO YOUR WHOLE HEALTH!

Your health is something you will not fully appreciate until it is gone. By age fifty, we have toasted to each other's health, have taught our children how to be healthy, and have always heard that when you have your health you have everything. Turning fifty presents us with one of two choices. Do we choose health or frailty? The choice is yours. You can choose right now to educate yourself on what you can do to help ensure that your fifth decade of life will be fabulous—body, mind, and spirit. The following chapters will unlock the secrets and tips you need to accomplish the goal of making your fifty the new thirty, redefining the aging process and living well as you do it!

At fifty, you need to practice "responsible self-care." Consider the following guidelines when implementing any suggestions contained in this book:

- Do not self-diagnose. If you have symptoms that suggest an illness described in this book, please consult your health care provider.

- If you are currently taking prescription medication(s), you must work with your doctor *before* discontinuing any drug, altering any drug regimen, or taking any supplements.

- Many nutritional supplements and herbal products are effective on their own, but they work best when they are used as a comprehensive natural approach to health that incorporates a healthy diet and lifestyle. Don't expect a supplement to save you from the consequences of continued poor lifestyle choices.

- While this book discusses the use of natural products for numerous midlife conditions, *it is not intended as a substitute for appropriate medical care.*

- Please work closely with your physician before implementing these antiaging suggestions—especially if you are on medications, as some nutritional supplements interfere with medications.

According to Ronald Klatz, MD, DO, who is the president of the American Academy of Anti-Aging Medicine, more than 75,000 people in the United States have reached 100 or older. Antiaging researchers predict that humans may soon be living to 120 or even 150 years of age! I'm sure this exciting information will motivate you to embark on your midlife voyage to vibrant health. This book will equip you with knowledge and antiaging protocols to help you be fabulous at fifty—and beyond.

Chapter 1

REDEFINING THE AGING PROCESS

Many of the situations that occur at fifty are uncontrollable. This is a time of life when you find out, maybe for the first time, that *you* are not in control. The good news is that reaching age fifty gives us a wonderful opportunity to develop and grow spiritually.

Age fifty can be a turning point for those who will use it as such. It is the time of life to take inventory of your life. It is the time to pay attention to the whispers that have been alerting you of the imbalances in your professional, personal, and family life, as well as your physical, emotional, and even financial health. It is a time to put your hands back on the wheel in terms of your life's course. It is a time to reflect on the past and what you have learned from it. It is the time to get rid of any baggage you are still toting on this earthly journey that may be weighing you down, such as debt, unforgiveness, anger, and personal relationships that take all your energy and rob you of being all you were meant to be.

At fifty, you must lighten your load—because a new load of issues awaits you at the next stop! Now more than ever, traveling light is important. Turning fifty can be a springboard to a new era in your life, complete with improved health, spiritual fulfillment, and long-lasting relationships that enrich your life. Strong relationships are key factors in surviving life after fifty. This is your wake-up call. Will you rise and meet the challenge?

In this chapter, I will discuss relationship issues that require extra attention by age fifty.

MIDLIFE MARRIAGE STRIFE

What makes a marriage last forever? Is it love, laughter, romance, or friendship? What makes a marriage fail? Indifference, selfishness, infidelity, financial strain? Whatever the answer, midlife is a time when all of the above apply. Midlife marriages fail at an alarming rate. Some make it—barely. But others not only survive; they thrive. What is their secret?

It has been shown that during midlife, many marriages fail because one or both spouses fail to meet the other's emotional needs. That is understandable, given the huge amount of stress and responsibility that often occurs during midlife. Couples may neglect to schedule time with one another. Their relationship is not a high priority. It is often replaced by activities of lesser importance, such as career, home maintenance, and financial worries.

This is dangerous to midlife relationships. You need time for each other, or you will never know the emotional needs of your spouse. Nor will you be able to avoid being the cause of each other's unhappiness. Time and undivided attention are critical components for everything that is important in a marriage. You and your spouse fell in love with each other because in some way you met each other's needs.

A safeguard against a midlife affair is to give each other the kind of attention you gave when you were dating: conversation, affection, recreational companionship, and more. When people have affairs at midlife, they give each other this kind of attention, so why not give it to your spouse? Why should his or her emotional needs get met in an affair that could lead to divorce?

Your marriage can be a lifetime love affair. Protect it by setting time aside each week to give each other undivided attention and appreciation. Pray together, stay together, and go the distance together. Happily married couples fare better at midlife than singles because of the important emotional connection and shared interests. When you meet each other's emotional needs, you become each other's source of happiness. You truly become one.

EMPTY-NEST SYNDROME

By age fifty, many midlifers are dealing with the empty-nest syndrome.

At age fifty, we experience many losses. We lose hormones, hair, and our car keys. When children leave home for college, marriage, or to move to an apartment to begin their lives, one thing is certain: there will be an empty quietness that fills the house, a reminder that a chapter in life has ended.

If you are married, this is not only a big adjustment for you, but it is also a major adjustment for even the best of marriages. For the first time in years, you will be forced to look closely at your marriage and its strengths as well as weaknesses. It is a time to discover each other all over again, to develop new shared interests. Sadly, many marriages crumble because they had been so consumed by child rearing and work that they lost touch with one another. These couples will be forced to examine where they will go from here. If both partners are going through the transitional years of andropause and menopause, as they often are, it can be especially difficult, given the irritability and fatigue that hormonal decline brings.

If you are a single parent, a supportive circle of friends is extremely important, as are close family ties. These will help a single midlifer deal with yet another unavoidable midlife change. When you are a single parent going through the empty-nest experience, one consolation is that there seems to be more freedom to make exciting new changes at this time of life. A single midlife parent may change careers, take classes, or get that degree he or she never finished. Such people may date for the first time in years, and maybe even marry. They may travel, paint, sing, or dance. There can be many firsts at age fifty. The possibilities are endless!

The empty-nest syndrome affects women much more than men due to the fact that women are natural-born nesters. When the nest is empty, women must find something else to nurture. Many women need to take this opportunity to nurture themselves at age fifty—*before* they begin the next chapter in their lives. It is a fact that both men and women are living longer these days. If you nurture yourself at fifty, you can revitalize your mind, body, and spirit and redefine the aging process. You must be willing to do the work. This will help ensure that your upcoming "golden years" are truly that.

MIDLIFE SQUEEZE: THE SANDWICH GENERATION

Today's fifty-year-olds are far and away the most stressed group in history. Our parents are living longer, and our children are putting off marriage and staying home longer or returning from college to live at home in order to save for the future. That leaves us stuck somewhere in the middle. We are literally sandwiched between the needs of our children as they begin their adult lives and the needs of our aging parents as they near the end of theirs. Just when we reach the time of life when we ought to be able to take a deep breath, we are needed by everyone near and dear to us, now more than ever!

This can be extremely overwhelming at a time when most marriages need some extra TLC, some catching up, and some rekindling time. In addition, menopause and andropause pack a wallop to our entire existence, leaving us worn out and lacking in coping skills. This is especially true if a person has burned the candle at both ends from a very young age.

Age fifty is also a time of loss. We are losing our hormones. Our parents may be unwell or dying, and our children are or will soon be gone to begin their own lives. Strangely enough, it is during this time of loss that many people find themselves again. Ask anyone who has experienced loss and is on the other side of the experience. Many times they will tell you that they were forced to return to the person they truly are. In other words, they no longer live their lives based upon others' expectations. They no longer live to please the world and other people, nor do they do things that they do not want to do. They have a stronger sense of self. They redefine themselves. Many have developed a strong prayer life during a season of loss. They emerge stronger, wiser, and more grounded than ever before.

By age fifty we receive the gift of realizing that we are more than this earthly frame. As the aging process becomes more evident during midlife, we see that we are not indestructible. While this may be humbling, it encourages many people to, perhaps for the first time, seek God to develop and cement their personal relationship with Him. Fifty-year-olds can find great comfort in the fact there is definitely a God who is more magnificent and loving than any person, place, or thing. At a time of life when so much loss occurs—whether it be through the death of a loved one, a divorce, an illness, or an emotional upheaval—this is a great blessing when being an active part of the sandwich generation takes a bite out of your life.

HERE'S HELP

There are about 22 million caregivers in American households who attend to the needs of elderly relatives or friends. The physical and emotional burden can take a serious toll. Being a caregiver as well as working, raising children, and giving attention to a marriage partner can accelerate your aging process as you watch someone you love slowly decline. By age fifty, you need to know when to ask for help.

Because this is the largest generation of caregivers, advocacy organizations called Area Agencies on Aging have been formed in all fifty states. They provide in-home training on how to manage loved ones who are wheelchair-bound or bedridden, and they also offer respite care. For more information, please visit their Web site at www.n4a.org or the Web site of the U.S. Administration on Aging at www.aoa.gov.

Family Caregiver Alliance's National Center on Caregiving has a Web site (www.caregiver.org) that offers fact sheets on different illnesses as well as online support for issues like caregiving frustration, problem behaviors, and how to balance family and work while caregiving. The Red Cross has implemented a nine-point program for caregivers at local churches, schools, and libraries. The program covers healthy eating, home safety, and general caregiving skills (www.redcross.org). The Alzheimer's Association has eighty chapters nationwide that offer educational programs on dementia, Alzheimer's, and related caregiving issues like stress and communication problems between patient, doctor, and caregiver (www.alz.org).[1]

SHOW ME THE MONEY

At age fifty, monetary management is quite different for us than it was for our parents' generation. Fifty-year-old women of that generation were brought up with the belief that they would always be taken care of by their husbands. With the help of life insurance policies and the enormous boom that occurred after World War II, many of them fared well. In addition, many of these same women never worked after they were married. Because their husbands were well insured, they never had to return to work even after they became widows.

Women today have come a long way and have been found to possess a keen knowledge for investing. This has opened a lucrative market for them in the financial industry. But there are far too many women, age fifty and older, who lack basic money handling skills and are overly dependent upon others, whether it be employers, husbands, or other family members.

It is at fifty that many unexpected life-changing events occur. Financial stability is another important piece to the midlife puzzle. Divorce, unexpected deaths, medical bills, financial emergencies, family members needing help—all of these can change your midlife nest egg into another type of empty-nest syndrome.

At fifty, having a sense of security about your finances is empowering and is actually believed to be associated with better health. This is probably due in part to the lack of financial worry that can manifest as anxiety and tension. At fifty, men and women have a duty to themselves to become financial experts. This may involve taking financial planning courses, meeting with a financial counselor or debt consolidator, or doing anything else that can strengthen your financial future.

Married midlife couples need to reexamine their past behaviors in respect to how they view money, with respect to spending, saving, and making it. They need to see where their differences are and together make future financial plans from a more unified perspective. At fifty it is imperative—whether you are married, widowed, divorced, or single—to plan for retirement and old age. Learn about investments instead of just spending and making money. If you take steps at age fifty in all of these areas, your financial portfolio will literally show you the money.

YOUR CHANGING BODY

Many experts agree that change is essential for a healthy second half of life. Instead of our focus being on career, child rearing, and other issues that consumed our younger years, longevity now holds the number one position on our priority list. Instead of feeling competitive pressure to reach the top of the corporate ladder, today's fifty-year-olds are becoming more accepting and relaxed about their accomplishments, and they are beginning to focus on retirement.

On the marriage front, the ones that have survived have become stronger and more stable after weathering the financial, hormonal, and child-rearing storms common to all marriages. The aging process and stress are constant companions that must be dealt with proactively on a daily basis. This is the main focus of this book.

Exercise is becoming the standard protocol at fifty, along with vitamins, minerals, and herbs targeted to specific body systems or particular health challenges. Daily UV protection in the form of sunscreens and sunless tanning creams have replaced the sun-worshiping mentality of our youth. Eye lifts, breast lifts, face-lifts, and hair transplants are becoming as popular as the hair dye our parents used to hold off the appearance of aging.

At fifty, you do not have the luxury of struggling against obstacles while being steeped in self-pity, substance abuse, anger, unforgiveness, or bitterness. Turning fifty can force a person to grow up in terms of emotional, physical, and spiritual health. The body is not as forgiving at fifty, as evidenced by morning stiffness after an evening of bending and lifting. Depression and anxiety from unresolved emotional issues can root even deeper if not dealt with and finally released.

Prayer and a strong spiritual life are essential to help marriage stress, improve sleep, melt anger and unforgiveness, and even lower blood pressure as a result. A rich spiritual life can help fifty-year-olds overcome any obstacle that comes before them. Grief, low self-esteem, depression, anxiety, weariness, and more can be taken to the One who made us. Once we do, we become new creatures. We are changed and free to live with the confidence that our joy will increase and our unhappiness will decrease along with all of the negative ramifications of these midlife problems.[2]

GOOD NEWS!

50 is the new 30
and
70 is the new 50

At fifty, wisdom is to the mind what health is to the body!

THE ERA OF SELF-HELP

Since age fifty brings so many physical, emotional, relational, and spiritual issues to the fore, the self-help industry has exploded. Oftentimes by age fifty we feel as if we need something—anything—to fix us, whether it be our weight, our marriage, our children, our appearance, our homes, or even just our continual need to fix something.

This explains the huge popularity of TV shows like *Dr. Phil, Oprah, Extreme Makeover,* and *Trading Spaces.* Sadly, as many fifty-year-olds can attest, self-help only offers short-term success. By age fifty, it is common to realize that we are not invincible. We are trapped in an earthly jacket of flesh and bones that is slowly but surely showing signs of wear. With each passing day we become more aware that there must be a purpose to our existence.

Those who have a relationship with their Creator have an assurance that although their earthly frame may be aging, there is a blessed hope. They realize that He has great plans for their future. They look forward with great anticipation to the day when they will no longer have to deal with pain, sickness, anxiety, depression, and sorrow. They know that no matter what this life may deal them, they are travelers passing through, not attached to this world and all of its earthly trappings. Further, they know that they are on their way to eternity. Because of that assurance, they fare better and react differently to problems that commonly besiege us at fifty.

Conversely, people who do not have a strong belief in a higher power seem to go into a freefall at midlife. They grapple with the meaning of life itself. As they see their youth slowly slipping away, they become depressed or downhearted. They may become fixated on preserving their looks by undergoing cosmetic procedures that give them only temporary satisfaction. They may be lonely as relationships change through divorce, illness, or death. They may harbor unforgiveness and anger over past hurts and decisions. Without a relationship with God, midlife can indeed be a scary, lonely, and bewildering time.

The good news is that by age fifty more people are open to a rebirth. They are searching for answers—that is a fact. Self-help cannot give them total comfort and assurance.

Strong relationships are the key to not just surviving but *thriving* during the fifth decade of life.

"Though no one can go back and make a brand-new start, anyone can start from now and make a brand-new ending."

—Carl Bard

Chapter 2

ZAPPING THE BIG EIGHT AGE-MAKERS

When John turned fifty, he noticed that his energy dropped drastically. In addition, every time he ate a meal he suffered from bloating and indigestion that sent him to the drugstore on a regular basis. He found himself catching every bug that circulated at his workplace. He also became concerned because his ability to focus and concentrate had diminished. John was experiencing what I call the new midlife crisis.

When I use the term *new midlife crisis*, I am referring to the alarming rate of degenerative diseases that occur to people in their middle years of life. The good news is that it is now believed that consuming the right supplements in the optimal dosages may greatly reduce a fifty-year-old's risk of developing cancer, Alzheimer's disease, arthritis, cataracts, and cardiovascular disease, and may redefine the aging process.

The following eight age accelerators should be addressed by all persons fifty and older. Once they are addressed, your chances of becoming fabulous at fifty are excellent! The following list names the eight main players involved in the aging process. I'll be explaining each one below and giving recommendations for preventing them.

1. Inflammation

2. Hormonal imbalance

3. Digestive enzyme deficiency

4. Oxidative stress

5. Fatty acid imbalance

6. Immune dysfunction

7. Excess calcification

8. Excitotoxicity[1]

Every fifty-year-old should be concerned about these eight age accelerators and should be taking steps to prevent or correct them. As I explain each condition below, I have outlined a supplement that can help deal with each one. By the end of this chapter, you will have a *protocol for antiaging* that every fifty-year-old should consider taking. Each recommended supplement is supported by research studies and thousands of clinical experiences by physicians around the world.

Inflammation

By age fifty, several lifestyle areas contribute to chronic inflammation, including diet, obesity, smoking, and a sedentary lifestyle. Chronic inflammation is related to most chronic disease processes, such as inflammatory disease of the skin, bowels, central nervous system, rheumatoid arthritis, allergies, asthma, atherosclerosis, cancer, and diabetes.

Curcumin is one of the most potent known anti-inflammatory agents.[2]

Curcumin (Turmeric)

Form: Capsule

Dosage: 500 mg

Frequency: Twice daily

Hormonal imbalance

Aging itself causes a hormonal imbalance that may be a contributing cause of many diseases associated with aging, such as osteoporosis, loss of libido, depression, and coronary artery disease (CAD). Simply taking lots of vitamins will not make you feel better if you suffer from a hormonal imbalance. You must restore the balance in your body. Youthful hormone balance is critical to maintaining health in women and men over age forty. The key to doing this is using bioidentical natural hormone supplementation.

Bioidenticals are hormone supplements that work with your body to enhance and reestablish your natural internal balance. Since they complement your natural hormones, your body accepts and uses them to reestablish your natural balance without the dangerous and uncomfortable side effects of synthetic hormones. Examples of bioidenticals would be natural estrogen or progesterone derived from plant sources such as soy or Mexican wild yam. Or you may use herbs like black cohosh and vitex that are standards in natural medicine.

To determine whether you need to take these supplements to restore your hormonal balance, you should have your doctor perform a formal assay (blood work) on you every year. The results of your assay will help your health care provider determine a hormone-balancing protocol tailored to your specific needs. This yearly assay will serve as a guide to insure that balance is achieved and maintained.

This assay should determine your levels of:

- DHEA sulfate

- Progesterone

- E1, E2, E3 (estradiol, estrone, and estriol)

- T3

- T4 (thyroid panel)

- TSH

- Testosterone

- FSH

- LH

Men should also have a PSA (prostate specific antigen) test done yearly. Women should receive Pap and pelvic exams yearly and, after age fifty, annual mammograms.

Note: For more information on male and female midlife hormone modulation, refer to my chapters on andropause, perimenopause, and menopause in Part II.

Digestive enzyme deficiency

The aging pancreas often fails to secrete enough digestive enzymes. The aging liver sometimes does not secrete enough bile acids. This can result in chronic indigestion that can lead to various digestive diseases such as gastroesophageal reflux disease (GERD), nausea, bloating, gas, and poor food assimilation.

If you have these symptoms, supplement with digestive enzymes. This will help eliminate digestive problems and boost nutrient assimilation, which will in turn boost your immune system. Take enzymes from a plant source at the beginning of each meal.

A digestive enzyme supplement should be broad spectrum so that it can facilitate the digestion of protein, fat, carbohydrates, fiber, and milk lactose. Enzymes taken with meals help to replace naturally occurring enzymes that are destroyed in highly processed and cooked foods.[3]

Digestive Enzymes

Form: Capsule

Dosage: 2 capsules of a broad-spectrum plant
enzyme formula

Frequency: With each meal

Oxidative stress

Aging causes a loss of endogenous antioxidants. This allows free-radical damage to escalate. Free radicals are chemically reactive atoms with unpaired electrons. They attack cells and cause cellular damage. This damage is caused by exposure to radiation, overexposure to sun, and exposure to cigarette smoke and toxic chemicals. Free-radical damage has been implicated with the aging process and the development of degenerative disease. It is therefore prudent to supplement with antioxidants, especially at midlife.

Alpha-lipoic acid (ALA) offers protective benefits against oxidative stress. It has been called the universal antioxidant because it works in both water and fat-soluble free radicals, which are often the cause of the damaging oxidative process. This ability to "quench" free radicals in both lipid (fat) and aqueous (water) environments makes it second to none. In addition, alpha-lipoic acid chelates metals, which means it helps the body eliminate ingested heavy metals, such as mercury and lead.

Biotin should be taken with alpha-lipoic acid. This is because ALA can interfere with biotin's activity in the body. Additional biotin is therefore needed when daily intake of ALA exceeds 100 mg. The recommended dosage of ALA is 250 mg, once or twice daily. People with a deficiency of vitamin B_{12} should not take alpha-lipoic acid.[4]

> **Alpha-Lipoic Acid**
>
> Form: Capsule
>
> Dosage: 250 mg with 2500 mcg of biotin (Note: mcg stands for micrograms.)
>
> Frequency: 1–2 times daily

Fatty acid imbalance

Fatty acids maintain cell energy output. The effects of a fatty acid imbalance may be felt as low energy, irregular heartbeat, painful joint degeneration, and other age-related conditions. Supplementation with fatty acids can suppress chronic inflammation.

Fatty acids are part of our makeup. They live in our healthy cells, muscles, nerves, and organs. They are essential for life—which is why they are called *essential* fatty acids. Sources of these essentials include oils from nuts, vegetables, and some fish. These are unsaturated healthy fats. Without proper levels of good fats, dangerous saturated fats from animal fats and dairy products will replace the good fats in our cells. The healthy fats include GLA (gamma-linolenic acid), DHA (docosahexaenoic acid), and EPA (eicosapentaenoic acid).[5]

Note: Do not take essential fatty acids if you are on anticoagulant medications. Also note that for optimal absorption, do not take these with fiber supplements.

> **Essential Fatty Acids**
>
> Form: Soft gelcaps
>
> Dosage: GLA, 450 mg; DHA, 500 mg; EPA, 750 mg
>
> Frequency: Twice daily with meals

Immune dysfunction

As we age, the immune system loses its ability to attack viruses, bacteria, and cancer cells as it could in years past. It is at midlife that the immune system often turns on its host (you) and creates auto-immune diseases, such as rheumatoid arthritis. Immune boosting is mandatory at midlife.

Modern research has validated what has been known for centuries: garlic can support the immune system by increasing natural killer cells. I recommend Kyolic garlic and olive leaf extract to support immunity and promote a healthy intestinal environment with plenty of beneficial bacteria. Several studies have demonstrated that components of garlic are immune boosters. Pharmaceutical-grade olive leaf extract contains the highest concentration of oleuropein. Oleuropein is a bitter compound isolated from the olive leaf. It is a powerful phyto-chemical that strongly supports the immune system. Olive leaf extract also provides natural protection and a healthy environment for cells without suppressing immune system function or harming beneficial intestinal microflora.[6]

Olive Leaf and Garlic

Form: Olive leaf, capsules; garlic, liquid extract or capsules

Dosage: Olive leaf, up to 500 mg daily; garlic, 1,000 mg capsules or ½ teaspoon liquid extract (taken with meals)

Frequency: Twice daily

Excess calcification

Aging disrupts calcium transport, resulting in calcium being deposited into the heart valves, brain cells, and the middle arterial wall—which can cause arteriosclerosis. Calcium is an essential nutri-ent in the maintenance of human bone integrity, but it is important to keep it out of the arterial walls. Calcium buildup on arterial walls can begin as early as the second decade of life and can continue throughout adulthood.

It has been revealed that vitamin K may help keep calcium in the bone, where it does a great job of building strong bones. [7]

Note: Do not take vitamin K if you are on anticoagulant medication. The recommended dose is 9 mg of K_1 (known as phylloquinone) and 1 mg of K_2 (called menaquinone). Taking 3 mg of boron will also aid in retaining calcium in bones.

Vitamin K

Form: Soft gelcaps

Dosage: K_1, 9 mg; K_2, 1 mg; boron, 3 mg

Frequency: Once daily

Excitotoxicity

Excitotoxicity occurs when the brain ages and loses control of its release of neurotransmitters, such as dopamine and glutamate. This can result in brain cell damage and destruction. This also causes brain aging and degenerative neurological disease. This can produce symptoms such as a loss of ability in thinking, remembering, and reasoning.

Vitamin B_{12} (methylcobalmin) is a brain cell protector. It has been shown to protect the brain against excitotoxic neuronal damage. Vitamin B_{12} comes in pill or liquid form. For best effectiveness, it should be dissolved under the tongue (sublingually) in order to bypass the liver during its first pass through the bloodstream. The dose for healthy midlifers is 1 mg, while the dose for those with neurological impairments is from 20–80 mg daily, depending upon severity of symptoms.[8]

> **Vitamin B$_{12}$**
>
> Form: Liquid or pill
> Dosage: Liquid, 1,200 mcg; pill, 1 mg
> Frequency: Once daily

ADDITIONAL MIDLIFE HEALTH INSURANCE

I suggest you also take a daily multivitamin and mineral supplement to ensure that you are filling all of the nutritional gaps left by our standard American diet. Look for a complete formula that offers broad-spectrum nutritional support using antioxidants, nutrients, and botanicals.

SUMMARY

- Have a yearly hormonal assay to determine if hormone replacement therapy is indicated.

- Use digestive enzymes from a plant source at each meal (one to two capsules).

- Take alpha-lipoic acid (250 mg) with biotin (2,500 mcg) up to twice daily to quench free radicals.

- Take DHA (450 mg), EPA (500 mg), and GLA (750 mg) fatty acids for broad-spectrum support in gelcap form.

- Take garlic (Kyolic liquid or capsules) and olive leaf (500 mg) up to three times daily.

- Take vitamin K$_1$ (9 mg), vitamin K$_2$ (1 mg), and boron (3 mg).

- Take vitamin B$_{12}$ sublingually (1 mg) in pill or liquid form.

CONCLUSION

In this chapter I have outlined a program of supplements that every fifty-year-old should consider. It will help *prevent* the onset of certain degenerative diseases, it will help to *restore* the body's youthful balance, and it will help to *manage* the uncomfortable conditions that commonly afflict fifty-year-olds helping to redefine the aging process.

I have said it already, but it bears repeating: please consult your physician before beginning this regimen. Your doctor needs to know what you are taking and how often, especially if you currently take prescription medications or have ongoing medical conditions for which you have been in a physician's care.

Fabulous Fifty Tip:

I take nothing for granted. I now have only
good days or great days!

Chapter 3

HEALTHY AGING: ADD MORE LIFE TO YOUR YEARS!

At fifty, our values have matured. What once greatly mattered may now seem trivial. We no longer sweat the small stuff!

There's a popular song that talks about growing old together because the best is yet to come. If that's so, why then at midlife do we have a culture that at all costs tries to stop visible signs of aging?

Maybe it's because we think that getting older signifies the end of an active life. We have less vitality mentally, sexually, and physically. In our youth-worshiping age, so much emphasis is placed on youth that plastic surgery is literally booming and making this once-Hollywood-only group of procedures now available to the average American—complete with convenient finance plans!

The truth is that it is the *quality* of our lives that is important. The health of the body, mind, and spirit create in us either an ageless glow or an old, haggard demeanor.

Guess what? Youth is not a chronological age, and advancing age is not the enemy—disease is! The good news is that our bodies can be rejuvenated at any age, thereby giving us healthier, vibrant years. We can slow the aging process by making sure we maintain the very best internal environment possible to prevent disease. While it is true that cell age is genetically controlled, disease or illness is most often the result of poor diet, lifestyle, and environment choices—not to mention stress!

Research in longevity has shown that there are three main causes of aging:

1. Enzyme depletion from poor diet and inadequate enzyme supplementation

2. Lowered immune response, which sets the stage for disease

3. Cell and tissue damage from free radicals

These three main causes of aging are included in the eight age accelerators discussed in chapter 2.

Remember, exercise is considered the best nutrient of all time. It can prolong fitness at any age; it helps increase stamina, circulation, and joint mobility; and it lifts depression. Exercise keeps you feeling young.

DO YOU HAVE ARTHRITIS?

When you are in pain, you don't want to rock the boat and make things worse. I recommend that you begin with deep breathing exercises daily. (Doing this outdoors in the morning is especially good.) In addition, stretching exercises will help to limber up the body in the morning, and at night before bed they will help relax you and promote a better night's sleep. You might also begin a walking program. You will be surprised at how great it makes you feel. Start slowly at first. As you continue, you will see that you can walk faster and for longer periods of time.

ARE YOU OVERWEIGHT?

Ten to thirty pounds of extra weight can take two years off your life. Thirty to fifty extra pounds can take off four years. And over fifty pounds of extra weight can take off eight years. You also have to consider all of the diseases associated with obesity—like diabetes, cancer, and arthritis. If you want to extend your lifespan, start losing that weight.

STOP SMOKING!

Nothing ages you more prematurely than smoking (with the exception of too much sun exposure). Smoking uses up tissue oxygen, which feeds the brain and helps prevent disease. Each cigarette takes eight minutes off your life. One pack a day takes one month off your life each year. Two packs take ten to fifteen years off your life. In addition, cigarettes have over 4,000 known poisons. You'll be interested to know that just one drop of nicotinic acid can kill a man.

ANTIAGING SELF-EXAM

Take this quiz to help determine if you are aging faster than necessary.

- Have you noticed brown spots on the back of your hands and around your eyes and nose?

- Is it more difficult for you to lose weight than it used to be?

- Do you have frequent indigestion, heartburn, or gas after eating a meal?

- Do you have insomnia?

- Do you have heart palpitations or chest pain?

- Do you have poor eyesight?

- Have you experienced hearing loss or ringing in the ears?

- Are you frequently constipated?

- Is your hair turning gray?

- Have you lost height?

- Is your skin becoming drier or thinner? Are you noticing more moles, bruises, or cherry angiomas (red blood blisters)?

- Is your recovery time slower from a cold or flu than it used to be?

- Do you have poor circulation?

AGING TOO FAST?

Elasticity test

This test measures the degree of deterioration of the connective tissue under the skin, which is a sign of aging. Pinch the skin on the back of your hand between your thumb and forefinger for five seconds, then time how long it takes to flatten out completely. Up to age fifty, it will take about five seconds. By age sixty, the average time is ten to fifteen seconds. By age seventy, it will take between thirty-five to fifty-five seconds.[1]

ANTIAGING OUTLOOK AT AGE FIFTY

1. Service—I involve myself in non-work activities that serve others, such as community service, charity work, or spiritual outreaches.

2. Responsibility—I take complete responsibility for my feelings and do not blame others.

3. Attitude—I am optimistic with a positive attitude that impacts the way I view life, the world, and the people I interact with.

4. Acceptance—I accept myself, including my faults and limitations. I do *not* expect perfection in my life.

5. Mental fitness—I keep my mind sharp through continuous learning. Mental challenges are regular and rewarding experiences for me.

ADD LIFE TO YOUR YEARS—WITH GOOD NUTRITION!

Here is a list of the all-time best longevity secrets.

- Drink plenty of pure water each and every day. This will keep you hydrated and help all of your body's systems work more efficiently. In addition, water will help proper elimination, remove toxins, and lessen arthritic pain. It also helps transport proteins, vitamins, minerals, and sugars for assimilation. Water helps the body work at its peak. Dehydration is one of the top ten causes of hospital stays among the elderly.

- Practice caloric reduction, too. As you age, your body requires fewer calories, and it burns calories at a lower rate. In addition, a low-calorie diet has been shown to protect your DNA from damage. This will thereby prevent organ and tissue degeneration.

- Try to get more "bang for your caloric buck" by eating only high-quality, densely nutritious foods at each meal, such as fruits and vegetables (fresh and locally grown, without the use of pesticides or herbicides, if possible).

- Avoid fried foods, red meat, too much caffeine, and highly spiced and processed foods.

- Eat fresh seafood at least twice weekly for thyroid health and balance.

- Have a green drink daily. (A green drink is a powdered drink mix that contains a natural combination of wheatgrass, barley, chlorella, brown rice, and kelp; this powder is mixed with juice or water.)

- Eat nuts, seeds, beans, and fiber—essential fatty acids are living nutrients.

- Go to the garden! Fresh fruits and vegetables are enzyme rich and full of vitamins, minerals, and fiber. They also give you the most minerals, vitamins, enzymes, and fiber. Plants give you easy-to-use, powerful nutrients for your body. Choose organic, and you will be assured of even higher nutrient content and lack of toxic sprays. In addition, juicing fresh fruits and vegetables offers even quicker absorption of powerful antioxidants, which protect the body from degenerative conditions, aging, heart disease, and cancer.

CHECK YOUR NUTRITIONAL STATUS AT FIFTY

- ☐ Fresh: I eat at least five servings of fresh fruits and vegetables every day.

- ☐ Colors: I choose a wide variety of fruits and vegetables from all parts of the color spectrum.

- ☐ Processed food: I avoid processed and fast foods whenever possible.

- ☐ Water: I drink six to eight glasses of water daily.

- ☐ Weight: My BMI (body mass index) and weight are within healthy guidelines.

TURN YOUR HOURGLASS UPSIDE-DOWN

⭐ *Starred supplement: Coenzyme Q$_{10}$*

Coenzyme Q$_{10}$ (CoQ$_{10}$) is a naturally occurring compound that is vital to the energy-producing core of all the body's cells. It is excellent for cardiovascular health, periodontal disease, and gum problems. CoQ$_{10}$ provides support to all cells of the body, and it is especially supportive of tissues that require a lot of energy, such as the heart muscle, periodontal tissue, and the cells of the body's natural defense system. CoQ$_{10}$ provides increased energy, exercise tolerance, and optimal nutritional support for the cardiovascular system.[2]

Coenzyme Q$_{10}$ (CoQ$_{10}$)

Form: Soft gelcaps

Dosage: 100 mg

Frequency: If you are under age forty, one capsule daily; if you are forty to fifty years of age or in ill health, one to two capsules daily; if you have heart conditions, you may take three to four capsules daily (under the supervision of a physician).

Second tier

It has been theorized that the following supplements may have antiaging benefits:

- Multivitamin/mineral supplement

- L-glutathione—antioxidant and amino acid that neutralizes radiation and inhibits free radicals

- Gotu kola—brain and nervous system health

- Royal jelly—antiaging superfood great for chronic fatigue and immune health; great source of pantothenic acid

- Lycopene—anticancer antioxidant; reduces the risk of prostate and cervical cancer

- Vitamins A, C, and E—antioxidants

- Bilberry—protects against macular degeneration

- Germanium—increases tissue oxygenation, thereby preventing disease

- Ginkgo biloba—helps restore circulation; improves hearing and vision; improves memory and brain activity

- Green superfoods—spirulina, chlorella, barley green, kelp, and wheatgrass

- Astragalus—for adrenal health; helps to lower blood pressure; improves circulation

- Reishi, shiitake, and maitake mushrooms—power mushrooms that boost immunity and may help prevent cancer; antiviral and antibacterial

- Hawthorn berry—protects the heart from free-radical damage; helps the heart pump blood efficiently

- Plant enzymes—sparks of life. As we age, we become enzyme depleted; supplementing with plant enzymes improves digestion, thereby enhancing all of our other body functions (elimination, assimilation, alertness, and energy levels).

- Red ginseng (for men)—an adaptogenic herb (an herb that provides energy to all body systems, promotes strength, fortifies the body against the effects of stress and fatigue, promotes testosterone production, and normalizes body function)

- White or American ginseng—helps to stimulate memory centers in the brain

- Siberian ginseng—supports the glandular system (especially the adrenals), circulation, and memory

- Yogurt or acidophilus—helps boost friendly bacteria in the intestinal tract; take daily for nutrient assimilation

- Laugh, be optimistic, play, and pray!

HEALTH UPDATES

In one study, people over the age of sixty-five who took multivitamins daily were found to be sick with infection related to illnesses only half as often as people who did not take vitamins.[3]

Another study shows that you can boost the antiaging powers of your next meal by adding fresh oregano. Shiow Wang, PhD, a scientist at the USDA's Agricultural Research Service, tested the antioxidant action of twenty-seven culinary herbs and twelve medicinal herbs. All varieties of oregano came out on top. Even more surprising was finding that oregano's antioxidant activity exceeded that of vitamin E![4]

Vitamin E slows aging

Researchers believe that vitamin E, when taken at the onset of middle age, will slow damage due to aging in the human brain and immune system. In a study in which middle-aged mice and old-aged mice were fed diets supplemented with vitamin E, normal age-related damage to vital proteins in their brain and immune system cells was delayed and even prevented.[5]

Estrogen—memory pill?

It is important to note that estrogen replacement therapy increases the risk for breast, uterine, and ovarian cancer over time. Women with a family history of any of these hormone-related cancers should not take estrogen. If you do take estrogen, take natural estrogen, and always only take it in consultation with your physician.

Latest discovery: HGH—human growth hormone

HGH, also known as somatotropin, is the hormone that regulates growth. When administered to older adults, it reduces fat tissue, rebuilds muscle mass, and helps to reverse changes that are associated with aging. Use HGH only under the guidance of your health care professional.

ENZYMES BOOST YOUR LONGEVITY POTENTIAL

Our life expectancy can be extended by ten to forty years. We must make sure that we are doing all we can to build health. That simply includes sleeping enough, de-stressing, making healthy food choices, and making sure that we are assimilating nutrients properly. Enzyme supplements help your body get the most out of the foods you eat. They help the body heal itself. According to DicQie Fuller, PhD, author of *The Healing Power of Enzymes,* midlife aging has a great deal to do with decreased enzyme reserves.[6]

Enzyme therapy slows down the aging process by building up enzyme reserves and quenching free radicals. Midlifers who suffer from diabetes, obesity, high cholesterol, high triglycerides, stress-related problems, and hormonal and digestive disturbances need enzyme supplementation.

Enzyme test

Most people derive great benefit from a full-spectrum plant enzyme formula. You may, however, look at the following chart to determine which enzymes you may need to start adding to your midlife health-building program. If you meet one or more of the conditions on one of these lists, consider adding that enzyme to your supplement regimen.

ENZYME DEFICIENCIES

Amylase deficiency	Skin breakout; rash Hypoglycemia Depression Mood swings Allergies PMS (women who are deficient in amylase may have more severe PMS symptoms) Hot flashes Fatigue Cold hands and feet Neck and shoulder aches Sprue (a chronic, chiefly tropical disease characterized by diarrhea, emaciation, and anemia and caused by defective absorption of nutrients from the intestinal tract) General inflammation
Protease deficiency	Back weakness Fungal conditions Constipation High blood pressure Insomnia Hearing problems Parasites Gum disorders Gingivitis
Lipase deficiency	Aching feet Arthritis Bladder problems Cystitis Acne Gallbladder stress Gallstones Hay fever Prostate problems Psoriasis Urinary weakness Constipation Diarrhea Heart problems

ENZYME DEFICIENCIES	
Combination deficiency	Chronic allergies Frequent common colds Diverticulitis

Note: If you suffer from one or more of the items on this list, consider adding a full-spectrum plant enzyme to your regimen. I recommend—and personally use—a broad-spectrum plant enzyme formula to cover all the bases: protease, lipase, and amylase.

LATEST FINDINGS ON HOW TO LIVE LONGER

Here are some of the latest findings from Dr. Michael Roizen, who introduced the Real Age concept—a scientific way of calculating a number that reflects your overall state of health rather than calendar age.[7]

- Use 9-inch plates—smaller plates means smaller portions. Age reduction equals 3.1 years.

- Eat fiber early in the day—fiber at breakfast slows the rate at which the stomach empties. This will help you not to snack and get excessive calories late in the day. Age reduction equals 0.6 years.

- Eat flavonoid-rich foods—green tea, broccoli, and strawberries can equal lower risk of breast and prostate cancer. Green tea has also been linked to a reduced heart disease risk. Age reduction equals 3.2 years.

- Combine vitamins C and E—they are more powerful when taken in combination. Age reduction equals up to 1 year.

- Get enough folate (a B vitamin)—it lowers homocysteine, an amino acid linked to heart disease. Age reduction
equals 1.2 years.

- Laugh more—it reduces stress, lowers cancer risk, and
lowers levels of heart disease, stress, and hypertension.
Age reduction equals 1.7 to 8 years.

- To calculate your real age, go to the Real Age Web site at
www.realage.com.

Fabulous Fifty Tip:

Eat less...live longer. Eat naturally,
and make sure your food does, too!

Chapter 4

BEATING STRESS
BEFORE IT BEATS YOU

Are you anxious about turning the big 5-0?

Excessive worry, tension, edginess, irritability, insomnia, disturbed sleep, fatigue, difficulty concentrating, rapid heartbeat (palpitations), shakes, chills, hot flashes, nausea, diarrhea, stomach pain, chest pain, shortness of breath, headaches, muscle aches, and back pain—all these are symptoms of persistent anxiety. At fifty, many people visit their physician for these life-disrupting symptoms. After running blood tests, EKGs, stress tests, and X-rays, most often the verdict comes back as stress.

Persistent anxiety can make it difficult for you to concentrate at work, function at home, or just live your life. Currently, more than 10 million Americans are leading troubled lives due to persistent anxiety. A variety of factors have been identified as possible causes of persistent anxiety. It has been shown to run in families, which indicates that there may be a hereditary link. At midlife, anxiety is often due to stressful life events. Anxiety takes its toll on your emotions and affects your body.[1]

According to the Midwest Center for Stress and Anxiety, persons who suffer from anxiety and/or chronic illness have common traits. They may have a tendency to overreact, are extremely analytical, have high expectations, worry about health problems, and have inner nervousness. In addition, they are often emotionally sensitive, perfectionists, and overly concerned about others' opinions of them. They tend to suffer from chronic "disease to please," always putting others first while neglecting their own need for rest, proper diet, and relaxation.

The following stress test will help you to assess your midlife stress load so that you may take steps to diffuse it. While there is no quick fix for persistent anxiety, relief is possible. Once you recognize the signs of stress and take action early enough through exercise, relaxation, dietary changes, and prayer, you will not fall victim to the destructive cycle of stress that robs you of your quality of life and well-being.

Stress Rating Scale

A score below 150 points means that you have a 30 percent chance of developing a significant health problem in the near future. A score between 150 and 300 points gives you a 50 percent chance of developing a significant health problem. A score of more than 300 points raises the possibility of significant health problems to a whopping 80 percent.[2]

Check off any items that apply to you, and then add up your total score at the end.

EVENT	POINT VALUE	YOUR SCORE
Death of spouse	100	
Divorce	78	
Marital separation	65	
Detention in jail	63	

EVENT	POINT VALUE	YOUR SCORE
Death of close family member other than spouse	63	
Major personal injury or illness	53	
Dismissal from job	47	
Marriage	50	
Marital reconciliation	45	
Retirement	45	
Major changes in health or behavior in family member	44	
Pregnancy	40	
Sexual difficulties	39	
Major business readjustment	39	
Major change in financial status	38	
Death of a close friend	37	
Change in occupation	36	

EVENT	POINT VALUE	YOUR SCORE
Change in number of arguments with spouse	35	
Going into debt for major purchase	31	
Foreclosure of mortgage or loan	30	
Major change in responsibility at work	29	
Son or daughter leaving home for college or marriage	29	
Trouble with in-laws	29	
Outstanding personal achievement	28	
Spouse begins or ceases work outside the home	26	
Beginning or ceasing formal schooling	26	
Major change in living conditions—for example, new home, remodeling, etc.	25	
Revision of personal habits	24	
Trouble with your boss	23	
Major change in working hours or conditions	20	

EVENT	POINT VALUE	YOUR SCORE
Change in residence	20	
Change in schools	20	
Major change in usual type or amount of recreation	19	
Major change in church activities	18	
Major change in social activities	18	
Taking a loan out for smaller purchases	17	
Major change in sleeping habits	16	
Major change in family get-togethers	15	
Major change in eating habits	15	

Does this help give you a better understanding of why you may be stressing out?

GABA AND STRESS

While it is possible to dramatically improve symptoms of anxiety through medications, those carry side effects that can affect quality of life. These medications can be of help for a short time, but total health—mental, physical, and spiritual—comes from replenishing, restoring, and rebuilding the brain, body, mind, and spirit. (See chapter 34 for information on replenishing the brain.)

Gamma-amino butyric acid (GABA) is the most widely distributed of all the inhibitory neurotransmitters in your brain. Many researchers believe it plays an important part in the regulation of anxiety.

In a sense, traumatic memories can be stored throughout your body. Your brain is not the only organ that suffers. Your stomach, skin, muscles, heart, skeletal system, and any other organ of your body may suffer as well—leading to ongoing stress. Since there are GABA receptors throughout your body, some researchers believe that taking GABA in the proper amounts can reduce the stress, anxiety, and tension in any of the areas of the body mentioned above.

Many of my clients who complained of stomach trouble also had some trauma connection that was unresolved. It is interesting to note that, according to Dr. Billie J. Sahley's research, there is a brain in your gut. The gut's brain is located in the lining of the stomach, esophagus, small intestine, and colon. The brain in your head communicates with the brain in your gut. Dr. Michael Gershon, a professor of anatomy and cell biology, reported in a *New York Times* article on January 23, 1996, that many gastrointestinal disorders like colitis, irritable bowel syndrome, and diverticulitis can originate from problems within the gut's brain.[3]

Diarrhea, nausea, and constipation—all common complaints these days—can be a result of prolonged anxiety, stress, or emotional pain. This is because the brain in your head communicates with the brain in your gut by way of neurotransmitters (such as GABA). Though GABA is normally abundant throughout this complex network of the mind and body, when its supply is deficient, both brains suffer and your body is flooded with uncomfortable, life-disrupting symptoms. So it is possible that your present midlife health is a direct result of your stress levels, anxiety, grief, anger, and unresolved conflict—and the resultant deficiency of GABA.

The following chart will show you just how much of an impact that anxiety and trauma, both past and present, can have in depleting your GABA supply, which will, in turn, start a chain reaction of stress-related body symptoms.

YOUR PROTOCOL FOR ANXIETY MANAGEMENT

⭐ Starred supplement: GABA

GABA is the main inhibitory neurotransmitter that restores the brain. Its function is to regulate anxiety, muscle spasms, depression, and chronic stress.

Note: GABA is best taken with magnesium (200 mg) and vitamin B_6 (at least 10 mg).

GABA

Form: Capsule (may be opened and dissolved in water; relief in 10–12 minutes)

Dosage: 750 mg, free form (i.e., not combined with anything else)

Frequency: Up to three times daily as needed (taken on an empty stomach)

TIPS FOR BEATING STRESS[4]

- *Simplify your life.* Take inventory of how you spend your time, money, and energy, and determine whether you really need everything you currently invest in. Can anything go, without sacrificing personal or family happiness? Cut unnecessary stressful activities out of your life. Say no the next time you are asked to take on a new responsibility if you are already overextended.

- *Get enough sleep.* Most people don't. If you have trouble falling asleep, an evening routine can help you. But stay away from caffeine, and don't exercise late in the day. Try to maintain a regular bedtime, adjusting it no more than an hour on weekends.

- *Eat well.* Besides choosing healthy foods, make mealtimes a pleasant social encounter. Celebrate family time by working together to plan the menu, set the table, and cook.

- *Exercise.* A good workout triggers chemical reactions in our bodies, enhances our moods, and makes us more fit to handle physical challenges. Your exercise doesn't have to be structured. Look for simple opportunities to move a little more—park farther from your destination for a longer walk, take the stairs instead of the elevator, and toss a ball with your children or grandchildren in the backyard.

- *Have fun.* Keep a good balance of work and play, of solitary and group activities. Sometimes we need time alone to gather our thoughts; sometimes we need people around to hug, listen to, or share ideas.

- *Maintain a support system.* Make sure your schedule accommodates time with loved ones. Think of recreational activities you can do with friends or family that don't cost much. If you struggle with a disease or circumstance, such as single parenthood, join a support group. Churches are a great place to find loving support.

- *Meditate and pray.* Find ways to focus energy on a meaning and purpose beyond your everyday life.

- *Keep your sense of humor.* Laughter releases tension. Look for what's funny in everyday life. Find classic comedies on television.

- *Be assertive.* Don't bottle up negative emotions and experiences. When you have a difficult message to deliver, describe the situation, express your feelings, specify your wants, and say it directly to the person involved. Write it down first and practice verbally, if that helps.

- *Be creative.* Indulge in enjoyable hobbies, whether they be painting, gardening, dancing, writing in a journal, or singing in a church choir or by yourself.

- *Give of yourself.* Finding a way to help someone in need is the best way to remind yourself to be grateful for what you might otherwise take for granted.

- *Pamper yourself.* It doesn't cost much to relax with an aromatherapy bath, a foot bath, or even a series of back rubs from your spouse.

MINIMIZING STRESS IN ALL THE CATEGORIES OF YOUR LIFE

Less midlife stress equals more long-term success. The following suggestions are stress busters for the main anxiety-inducing areas of your life.

General tips

- Exercise with a workout buddy.

- Schedule a weekly massage.

- Fully express your appreciation and gratitude to someone who has helped you.

- Go over your calendar and schedule at least one stress-relieving session each week (lunch with a good friend, a date to catch a movie, etc.).

- Forgive anyone of anything negative you have been holding on to; you will be surprised at just how much energy will return once you let go of unforgiveness.

Money

- Cut up all but one of your credit cards. Pay them off by putting maximum payments against the highest rate card while making minimum payments on lower rate cards. Repeat until you are debt-free!

- Arrange for an automatic deposit from your checking account to a savings or investment account.

- Tithe to a church or charitable organization.

Home

- Create an ideal sleeping environment: dark and peaceful, comfortable bedding, and *no television*!

- Improve both water and air quality. Install water filters for drinking water and showers, as well as an air-cleaning system of some kind.

- Declutter your wardrobe: rid yourself of circa-1970 bell-bottoms, polyester slacks, platform shoes, and anything that does not fit or flatter. The rule of thumb is, "If it is in style again, you are too old to wear it."

- Switch to nontoxic cleaning supplies.

Just say no

At fifty, you have permission to act like a two-year-old and just say *no*.

Do you have the "disease to please"? This "illness" is one of the biggest stressors we face in life. That is, attempting to please *everyone*! Peace and calm come to us when we feel in control, while chaos occurs when we overcommit, leaving us overwhelmed and, therefore, stressed. At age fifty, you *must* learn how to acknowledge your limitations and your need for peace if you have not already done so. This way you can lower your stress levels and reclaim control over your life.

Remember back when you were two years old and how powerful you felt when you said no?

Fabulous Fifty Tip:

It isn't the load that breaks us down; it's the way we carry it!

Chapter 5

THE PAUSE THAT
REFRESHES—SLEEP

S leep deprivation clouds your thoughts, changes your personality, and ages you faster than time itself. One of the most powerful midlife rejuvenators costs you nothing, but many midlifers would pay just about anything for it—a night of sweet, sound sleep.

At age fifty, sleep is elusive for a number of reasons. For women, hormonal changes at menopause bring hot flashes and night sweats. And andropause sends men on nightly treks to the bathroom for frequent urination. Add to these the typical midlife conditions of anxiety, depression, illness, or chronic pain. Other possible causes of sleeplessness include the use of decongestant medications, cold remedies, antibiotics, appetite suppressants, contraceptives, and thyroid medications. Deficiencies in potassium and the B vitamins, so common in midlife due to stress or chronic pain syndromes, may also be a factor in the poor sleep picture.

Whatever the cause, it is vital to our well-being to sleep soundly because it is only during rest that our bone marrow and lymph nodes produce substances to empower our immune systems. Furthermore, it is during the beginning of our sleep cycle that much of the body's repair work is done. Asian medicine recognizes the importance of sleep, even suggesting that one hour of sleep *before* midnight is worth two hours of sleep after midnight, in terms of regeneration and healing.

Many fifty-year-old women tell me that they would love to be able to sleep as soundly as they did before they had children. Declining hormone levels may be responsible, as well as the fact that motherhood conditions us to become light sleepers. As children become teens, both mothers and fathers often keep an all-night vigil, waiting for their kids to return home safe and sound from their evening escapades. Often it's well after midnight, which leaves only a few hours until dawn to drift off to dreamland.

Sleep is a supreme tonic. It is important that you take steps to sleep deeply and restoratively. You need to determine and change the cause of your insomnia. If you are taking prescription sleep aids, you should know that sleeping pills impair calcium absorption, are habit forming, and may paralyze the part of your brain that controls dreaming. Many times they can leave us feeling less than rested and impair the clarity of our thoughts.

While trying to reestablish a healthy sleep pattern, there are a few rules. First, avoid caffeinated items such as coffee, tea, sodas, and chocolate. You should also avoid late-night eating. It has been said that sleep doesn't interfere with digestion, but digestion interferes with sleep. If you do eat late, choose a food that will promote relaxation like plain yogurt (which is rich in sleep-inducing tryptophan), oatmeal (which tends to promote sleep), turkey, bananas, tuna, or whole-grain crackers. Try a cup of chamomile tea, which is considered to be a nerve restorative and helps quiet anxiety and stress. This is probably due to the fact that it is high in magnesium, calcium, potassium, and B vitamins.

CHECK YOUR REST QUOTA

☐ Sleep—I sleep soundly through the night, getting at least seven to eight hours of sleep nightly.

☐ Work—I minimize excessive work hours. I determine the time I will go home at the beginning of the day and stick to it.

☐ Rest—once a week, I take a day of rest in which I do not do my regular work and instead focus on rest, relationships, inspiration, and attitude.

☐ Vacation—at least once or twice a year, I take a vacation that allows me to slow down or get away from it all in order to relax and rejuvenate.

YOUR PROTOCOL FOR REFRESHING SLEEP

⭐ *Starred supplement: Passionflower*

Passionflower helps relax the mind and muscles. It is an antispasmodic, sedative, and non-drowsy sleep aid.

> **Passionflower**
> Form: Tincture or capsule
> Dosage: 30 drops (tincture); 500 mg (capsule)
> Frequency: Once daily, 30 minutes before bed

⭐ *Starred supplement: Valerian*

Valerian helps anxiety-related sleep disorders.[1] Valerian has a strong odor that many people object to, so it is not usually desired as a tea. Some people may feel groggy or experience a "hangover effect" from valerian. If this happens to you, passionflower may be a better choice to help improve your sleep.

Warning: Do not combine valerian or passionflower with tranquilizers or antidepressant medications. If you are taking these medications, be sure to talk to your health care provider before you take any dose of valerian.

Valerian

Form: Tincture, capsule, or tablet

Dosage: 30–60 drops (tincture); 300–500 mg (capsule or tablet)

Frequency: Once daily, 30–60 minutes before bed

Second tier

It has been theorized that the following supplements may have beneficial effects for this condition of midlife:

- Hops—helps to induce sleep and is a safe and reliable sedative

- Melatonin—a natural hormone that promotes sound sleep

- DHEA—a natural hormone that improves the quality of sleep

- L-theanine—an amino acid that, if taken thirty minutes before bed, promotes deep muscle relaxation

- Calcium—has a calming effect and, when combined with magnesium, feeds the nerves

- Magnesium—relaxes muscles and, with calcium, feeds the nerves

- Inositol—enhances REM (rapid eye movement) sleep, the stage of deep sleep at which dreaming occurs

Lack of sleep robs your body of essential downtime necessary to rebuild vital organs and recharge your nervous system. People who return from a restful vacation will say they feel rejuvenated. Friends and co-workers will usually comment on how rested and relaxed they appear. Just think: if it is so evident on the outside, imagine what has taken place inside the body, mind, and spirit.

Refreshing sleep at fifty…it's a good thing!

Fabulous Fifty Tip:

"[Sleep is] the golden chain that ties health and our bodies together."

—Thomas Dekker

Chapter 6

MOVE IT OR LOSE IT—EXERCISE FOR LIFE

Our bodies were designed to move—to stretch, run, walk, jump, and play. By age fifty, getting out of bed or getting off the couch on the weekends may be a chore. This is mostly due to inactivity, stress, poor dietary habits, depression, fatigue, low adrenal function, and lack of quality sleep.

We are living in an era when physical labor is not the norm. We live in a fast-paced, high-tech society where exercise must be a planned activity. Most of us do not farm land, milk cows, mow the back forty, or dig wells. We have reached an era of computerized washing machines, dishwashers, and now even a robotic vacuum cleaner that vacuums the house on a continual basis.

We are more advanced technically but more unhealthy physically than our grandparents were at fifty. They experienced stress-relieving physical work that left them tired but satisfied at the end of each day. This differs from midlifers today, who remain wired and tired day in and day out.

At fifty, exercise is a tonic with miraculous effects on mood, weight gain, energy levels, and sleep quality. In addition, exercise boosts immunity, is a natural appetite suppressant, improves HDL (the good cholesterol), creates pain-relieving endorphins, strengthens midlife bones, lowers the chance of cardiovascular disease, and improves circulation and respiration.

At midlife, backs ache, neck and shoulders are tight, knees may creak, and hips hurt. Without regular exercise, we become unable to deal with physical stress. Fifty-year-olds have a hard time believing that the simple act of bending wrong or getting out of bed too fast can bring on a strained back or pulled muscles.

The sooner you begin to nurture and care for your fifty-year-old frame, the more comfortable this passage of life will be.

CHECK YOUR ACTIVITY AT FIFTY

☐ Movement—I take every opportunity to increase my daily movement (walking instead of driving, taking the stairs instead of the elevator, etc.)

☐ Aerobic—I get thirty to sixty minutes of aerobic exercise, such as walking, running, swimming, cycling, etc., three to six days per week.

☐ Strength—I have a muscle workout routine that challenges me at least three times per week, such as weight lifting, core strengthening, etc.

☐ Stretching—I have a stretching routine I do at least three times per week.

☐ Support—I have an exercise partner or friend that encourages me and keeps me accountable, which in turn makes the activity more pleasurable.

Fabulous Fifty Tip:

Bicycle for your life cycle!

Chapter 7

SOUL FOOD FOR
FIFTY AND UP

You are a spiritual being who is having an earthly experience. Therefore, just as you nourish your body, you must feed your soul and nurture your spirit.

Arriving at age fifty may lead you to self-examination. It may force you to take a deeper look at your life. Old, well-rooted beliefs may be unearthed and discarded. And, maybe for the very first time, unbelief may be challenged or replaced with faith.

At fifty, more than ever, your spiritual health and personal faith in your Creator is the life-giving tonic that is hidden from the rest of the world. With daily cultivation and connection to God, you will experience the inner peace and ability to cope with life's challenges.

Being fifty has a positive side made up of two very strong beliefs. First, you must have faith that your Creator has a plan and purpose for your life. Second, you must have faith that your Creator will work your trials out for your ultimate good, regardless of how your situation may look.

At fifty trials can grow us, forming us into stronger, wiser, better people. It is all in how you perceive it. You still need to take care of your physical body, devote quality time to relationships, and focus on all of the other aspects of midlife that need attention. And yet you can rest in the fact that even though midlife is a challenge to you, testing your armor and sometimes leaving you grappling with the very meaning of your existence, you need not view it from a defeated perspective.

Spend time in prayer and meditation daily, and live a life of service and love unconditionally. By doing so you will add stress-free years to your life. Use your midlife experiences as catalysts for turning your hourglass upside down and redefining your aging process.

CLEANING HOUSE

Why do some people sail through midlife virtually unscathed while others are weighed down with financial worries, relationship troubles, illnesses, and more? The answer could be that troubled people may be harboring unforgiveness, bitterness, anger, and resentment. When these pollutants are buried deep within our souls, they need to be purged. Self-examination exposes them.

Many times our loudest wake-up call comes at age fifty in the form of a meltdown. Like a pitcher of ice water poured on our midlife morning face, the Creator can use a meltdown to get our undivided attention. It is at age fifty that we are brought to a place where we need to change our behavior or beliefs. It is often at fifty that we are forced to get back to the real person we were meant to be. Midlife trials have a way of stripping us completely of pride, ego, materialism, and anything that is driving us away from our full potential.

Age fifty is the time for us to rekindle or strengthen our relationship with our Creator. Sometimes it takes a "midlife crucifixion" for us to run back to God. This allows us to be glorified as a reflection of the Creator's active work in our lives. It will become evident to those around you. Midlife transformations can leave you fully transformed, fully filled with the Creator's love and presence, and fully ready to live eternally.

Being fifty can force you to prioritize your life. Health, family, relationship with God, and peace of mind are the things that truly matter in this life. Turning fifty may be a little uncomfortable, but I encourage you to use your midlife trials as an opportunity to examine your life and find ways to become more positive of the fact that the Creator still is the sculptor of your life.

Turning fifty can compel us to embrace our spirituality. Many of us long for supernatural restoration by the grace of God. It is not a religion; it is a regeneration. When it occurs, it is radical. It is passionate. It is truth. Your spirit will know and recognize this. It is like coming home. When this occurs, especially during midlife and all of its trials, you will enjoy and take comfort in the fact that you will have fellowship with your Creator.

And fellowship with your Creator equals true happiness. Many great men before us confessed that without God life was meaningless. With God, the possibilities were endless. Empires have been conquered and wars have been won when, to the natural mind, such outcomes seemed like impossibilities. These great men of old knew from whence their help came.

Fabulous Fifty Tip:

Feed your spirit. You are a spiritual being having an earthly experience!

Part II

ANTIAGING/DISEASE-PREVENTING PROTOCOLS

ANTIAGING/DISEASE-PREVENTING PROTOCOLS

Part II of this book covers a wide array of conditions we may face at age fifty that can age us prematurely. I have set up this section in a user-friendly format so that you can look up your particular symptom or condition and go straight to that chapter for help.

At fifty, if you fail to plan, plan on failing health! Making your fifty feel like thirty requires planning on your part. Health and longevity do not come about on their own. You must become proactive to stem the tide of aging. You must set up your own personal goals and make them realistic, then implement the protocols in this book. Work daily toward fulfilling them. It is your journey. It is not a race! You are only limited by yourself. There is *no* limit to how healthy, how well, and how energized you can feel!

First let's begin with the three top not-so-secret tips to help make your fifty fabulous.

1. Exercise—of the three components, exercise is the *most* important one.

2. Diet—food is fuel. The kind of fuel you put into your fifty-year-old body can determine how well your body runs, recovers, and ultimately lasts!

3. Rest—sleepless nights increase the speed of the aging process.

Neglecting any one of these areas will lead to loss of performance, accelerated aging, and poor health.

Let's break it down. Exercise cuts down mortality rates at any age, but at age fifty the protection grows stronger with each passing day. This is truly a case of "better late than never." Your diet provides you with your energy source. Food supplies fuel to run your entire body, giving it the energy to perform its many functions and allowing you to do what you want and need to do. And without proper rest, our performance, length, and quality of life will suffer. Each one of these three great life extenders will be discussed in the following chapters.

Next you will notice that there are quite a few supplements recommended in this section. Start with the recommended supplements from chapter 2, and then use the approach I outlined in the introduction. Add one to two starred supplements to your existing regimen, and give them time to see if they help you. If they don't, you may simply add one or two more until you find the ones that help you. Always begin with the starred supplements for each condition before moving to the second tier—and always do this process in consultation with your physician.

Do not let the list of suggested supplements overwhelm you. Try them, and take time to feel the results in your body. There is real science behind this information. The research has been done for you. It is yours for the taking.

My goal is to educate and arm you with knowledge on how to redefine the aging process. This section will help you address specific conditions that affect millions of us by age fifty.

WHAT'S SWIMMING IN YOUR GENE POOL?

Before we begin I want to say that if your ancestors lived long lives, then you are truly blessed. But this does not mean that you can be complacent. For most of us, the deadliest diseases in our world today—heart disease, diabetes, stroke, and cancer—can be found in our family tree. So, in order to help prevent you from developing these diseases to which you may be genetically susceptible, you must do a little detective work and delve into your family's medical history.

RELATIONSHIP	CURRENT HEALTH ISSUES OR CAUSE OF DEATH
Mother	
Father	
Brother(s)	
Sister(s)	
Maternal grandmother	
Maternal grandfather	
Paternal grandmother	
Paternal grandfather	

The good news is that in our lifetime (the past fifty years), as I mentioned earlier, the human life span has increased dramatically due to earlier detection and treatment. If you find out that your ancestors died prematurely of one of the above-mentioned medical conditions, do not be alarmed. There is a *very* good chance of a modern cure! Remember, thanks to early detection, "to be forewarned is to be forearmed."

Chapter 8

GETTING TO THE HEART OF THE MATTER—
CARDIOVASCULAR HEALTH

Coronary heart disease (CAD) is the most common form of heart disease. It is caused by atherosclerosis and is characterized by a hardening and/or thickening of the arteries. It involves the slow buildup of deposits of cholesterol, calcium, fibrin, and cellular waste products. Combined, these substances create plaque that may partially or totally block the blood's flow through the artery. In addition, this buildup process may contribute to the development of a blood clot. Either one of these scenarios can result in a heart attack or stroke.

After age fifty, CAD can progress rapidly, so it is wise to take inventory now to see if you are at risk. There appear to be three basic and equally important probable causes of the disease process: homocysteine overload, low-density lipoprotein oxidation, and abnormal platelet aggregation. Homocysteine overload can cause abnormal arterial blood clots as well as excessive accumulation of arterial plaque and resultant arterial blockage. Low-density lipoprotein (LDL) oxidation is oxidation that makes LDL sticky and causes it to build up on the lining of blood vessel walls. Abnormal platelet aggregation (PA) can contribute to the development of a blood clot, which can lead to sudden death, heart attack, or stroke.

The good news here is that with appropriate diet, lifestyle, and exercise—coupled with targeted supplementation—we can help prevent and even help reverse cardiovascular disease.[1]

MIDLIFE HEART DISEASE: KNOW YOUR RISK

- Age (over forty-five in men and over fifty-five in women)

- High cholesterol

- High blood pressure

- Diabetes

- Family history of heart disease

- Being overweight

- Inactivity

- Smoking, either currently or in the past

- A diet high in cholesterol or saturated fat

Some factors are beyond our control, such as age and family history. Others are controllable with lifestyle modifications, such as eating a low-fat diet, exercising more, ceasing to smoke, and decreasing stress as much as possible.

THE NEW HEART TEST

Medical science now offers HeartScore, which is a CT scan that measures calcium deposits in the coronary arteries. Calcium is one component of plaque, which is the main culprit behind coronary artery disease and most heart attacks. Studies show that heart CT scanning is most useful for people with no CAD symptoms but at least one risk factor. The test is noninvasive, painless, involves no dye injection, and takes only a few minutes.

RECOGNIZE THE SYMPTOMS OF HEART TROUBLE

- Chest pain

- Shortness of breath

- Fatigue

HEART ATTACK SYMPTOMS

- Chest pain

- Pressure or tightness in the chest that lasts for more than a few minutes or that comes and goes

- Pain or discomfort in the jaw, neck, back, stomach, or either arm; shortness of breath; nausea; sweating; and anxiety

Call 911 if any of these symptoms develop!

YOUR PROTOCOL FOR HEART HEALTH

⭐ *Starred supplement: Coenzyme Q_{10}*

Coenzyme Q_{10} (ubiquinone), also called CoQ_{10}, has no known toxicity or side effects and has been the topic of numerous studies all over the world. It is a fat-soluble, vitamin-like substance that is involved in energy production within a cell. In addition, it is an antioxidant. A study in 1990 showed that 150 mg of CoQ_{10} reduced angina attacks by 46 percent and improved the capacity of physical performance.[2]

Coenzyme Q_{10} (CoQ_{10})

Form: Gelcap

Dosage: 100 mg

Frequency: For healthy young people, 1 capsule daily; for those in ill health or ages forty to fifty, 1–2 capsules daily; if you have heart conditions, 3–4 capsules daily (under the supervision of your physician)

Statin drugs (cholesterol-lowering medications) have proven in clinical trials to deplete coenzyme Q_{10}, the "spark plug" of the human body. In a citizen petition before the U.S. Department of Health and Human Services, physician and best-selling author Julian Whitaker wrote, "Patients who take statin drugs without coenzyme Q_{10}, particularly those with a history of heart disease, are especially prone to developing complications that can have fatal consequences." [3]

Dr. Whitaker also wrote that a deficiency of CoQ_{10} is associated with impairment of myocardial function; liver dysfunction; and myopathies, which include cardiomyopathy and congestive heart failure. Therefore, all patients taking statin drugs should be advised to take 100–200 mg of CoQ_{10} daily.

⭐ Starred supplement: B vitamins

Homocysteine levels can be normalized by supplementation with moderate doses of B vitamins—B_6, B_{12}, folic acid, and trimethylglycine (TMG, or betaine).[4]

Vitamins B_6, B_{12}, Folic Acid, and TMG

Form: Tablet or capsule

Dosage: B_6, 75 mg; B_{12}, 500 mcg; folic acid, 800 mcg; TMG, 1,000 mg

Frequency: Once daily

Second tier

It has been theorized that the following supplements may have beneficial effects for this condition of midlife:

- Vitamin E—according to the *American Journal of Clinical Nutrition* (August 1996), high-potency antioxidant supplements can reduce atherosclerosis in humans. The study showed that vitamin E reduced the risk of death from all causes in 11,178 elderly people from 1984 to 1993. Vitamin E supplementation also resulted in a 63 percent reduction in death from heart attack and a 59 percent reduction in cancer deaths. A study of 11,348 persons over a ten-year period found that high vitamin C intake prolonged average life span and reduced the death rate from cardiovascular disease by 42 percent.[5]

- Artichoke extract—has favorable effects on heart disease and arteriosclerosis; it can significantly decrease cholesterol levels.[6]

- Ginger extract (not to be confused with wild ginger, which can be hazardous)—scientists call ginger extract a "cardiotonic"; it helps to inhibit abnormal platelet aggregation.[7]

- Gugulipid—produces a blood fat lowering effect with no side effects. According to one journal, in patients with high blood fat levels, serum cholesterol declined by 21.5 percent and triglycerides by 27.1 percent after three weeks of gugulipid use; after sixteen weeks, HDL cholesterol (the good cholesterol) increased by 35.8 percent.[8]

- Magnesium—plays an important role in the health of the cardiovascular system.

- TMG (trimethylglycine)—extracted from sugar beets; helps to lower dangerous homocysteine levels, which in turn lowers the risk of heart disease and stroke.

- Alpha-lipoic acid—helps to combat oxidative stress, which plays a role in the development and progression of heart disease.

- Garlic—prevents abnormal blood clot formation inside blood vessels. According to one study, liquid garlic extract (Kyolic) caused a 12–31 percent reduction in cholesterol levels in the majority of test subjects after six months.[9] Garlic may also prevent the oxidation of LDL cholesterol as well as reduce blood platelet stickiness.

- Curcumin—derived from the yellow spice turmeric, curcumin prevents abnormal blood clot formation[10] and reduces cholesterol.[11]

- Aspirin—low doses of aspirin (81 mg) have been shown to be beneficial in the prevention of heart attacks and strokes. The American College of Chest Physicians recommends aspirin for all people over the age of fifty with one risk factor and no conditions that make aspirin use inadvisable, such as high cholesterol, diabetes, family history of heart attack or stroke, high blood pressure, and cigarette smoking.

- Omega-3 oils—reduce the incidence of atherosclerosis, second heart attacks, and strokes. Studies suggest that 3–4 grams of omega-3 oils per day provide protective effects against coronary heart disease. Fish, flax, and perilla oils are rich sources of omega-3 fatty acids. Perilla oil does not cause stomach upsets, which may make it a better choice for those persons with sensitive stomachs. In addition, it alleviates chronic inflammation, maintains cardiac cell energy output, and inhibits abnormal blood clotting. It also decreases PAF (platelet-activating factor), a major cause of heart attacks and stroke.[12]

To summarize, the keys to improving cardiovascular health are antioxidant protection, managing the effects of stress, strengthening the heart and vessels, and reducing the occurrence of calcification.

Chapter 9

DO I LOOK FAT?

At fifty, everything starts to slow down: stamina, hair growth, thinking, and metabolism. Weight gain in a fifty-year-old can set the stage for some of the most serious health threats of our time, including cancer, heart disease, and diabetes. When you add stress, which can result in excess cortisol production, you may gain twenty or so midlife pounds that seem impossible to lose.

YOUR PROTOCOL FOR WEIGHT MANAGEMENT

✪ Starred supplement: CLA

Do you consume too many carbs? Is your willpower lacking? This is very common at midlife, because carbs simply make us feel good and give us a quick fix when we are in a slump. But the key here is that a quick fix can turn into quick fat. The good news is that there may be an unrecognized reason why so many midlifers are obese. Thousands of Americans have adopted the low-carb, high-protein diet, which consists of foods like cheese, dairy, and beef, and they are seeing significant weight loss as a result. But Americans are having trouble keeping the weight off. The reason may be that a certain something is missing from the American diet.

That certain something may be conjugated linoleic acid (CLA). CLA's job is to take the fats we consume and convert them into muscle and energy. Without it, dietary fat is stored as new fat cells. Recent studies have suggested that CLA, taken as a supplement, can be used as a midlife weight management tool because of its ability to reduce body fat and maintain lean muscle mass.[1] A blind, randomized study in humans showed a decrease in abdominal fat after just four weeks of CLA use.[2]

Our bodies do not make CLA on their own, so we must obtain it from our diet. The problem is that the CLA content of the food in America (beef, dairy, and milk) has fallen to almost zero since 1950. It was during 1950 that farmers began feeding their cattle and dairy cows in feedlots rather than allowing them to graze in pastures. As a result, by the 1990s the CLA content of U.S. milk was less than 1 percent. It is interesting to note that in Australia, where cattle are still allowed to graze in pastures, the CLA content of pasture-fed beef is a whopping 400 percent.

Could this be a factor in the obesity epidemic in America that started in the 1950s? I think it is possibly a key player, especially since prior to the Atkins craze many Americans consumed less beef and dairy as they tried to slim their waistlines, but ended up becoming heavier because they were missing out on CLA, which in turn made it harder for them to lose weight.

Since the natural sources of CLA are low, the best solution is to supplement your diet with CLA. In both men and women, CLA can contribute to a body fat reduction of approximately 20 percent in as little as twelve weeks.[3]

CLA

Form: Capsule

Dosage: 1,000 mg

Frequency: Three times daily; do not take in
the late afternoon or evening as it may cause
sleeplessness

⭐ *Starred supplement: Relora*

For stress-related weight gain, there is another relatively new, patented formula called Relora. It is all-natural and has been found to be effective in the alleviation of irritability, emotional ups and downs, restlessness, tense muscles, poor sleep, and concentration difficulties associated with stress and anxiety. Best of all, Relora may help control stress eating, which is so common at midlife. The formula contains extracts from magnolia officinalis and phellodendron amurense, which have a long history of use in traditional Chinese medicine. When combined, they may help reduce the negative effects of stress.[4]

When the body is under stress, it causes the release of cortisol and specific stress hormones that influence mood and emotional well-being. A large percentage of overweight adults have excessive abdominal fat due to stress-related overeating. Relora may help maintain healthy levels of cortisol and DHEA in stressed individuals, induce relaxation, and act as an aid in controlling weight.[5]

Clinical studies with Relora have shown a 37 percent reduction in cortisol and a 227 percent increase in DHEA. In human trials with Relora, eight out of ten people were more relaxed, seven out of ten enjoyed more restful sleep, and nine out of ten people reported that Relora was gentle on the stomach.

Relora

Form: Capsule
Dosage: 250 mg
Frequency: Three times daily

Second tier

It has been theorized that the following supplements may have beneficial effects for this condition of midlife:

- Flax oil—fights midlife fat; similar to CLA, flax can make your body a fat-burning machine

- Creatine—stimulates muscle growth throughout the body; works best if you take it while implementing an exercise program at the same time

- Green tea—taken with meals, it can help burn up to 80 calories from fat

Chapter 10

DIGESTIVE HEALTH

Heartburn, gastroesophageal reflux disease (GERD), acid reflux, indigestion, bloating, gas, constipation, fatigue...such are the midlife menaces that plague thousands of fifty-plus-year-olds. Another robber of midlife health is poor digestion. When digestion is not optimal, energy is reduced and constipation, bloating, gas, reflux, allergic reactions, and nausea can be constant companions.

If poor digestion becomes chronic, you will find yourself joining the ranks of thousands, if not millions, of midlifers reaching for Tums, Rolaids, and, more recently, Nexium and Prilosec, as well as the good old "pink stuff." These medications only suppress the underlying problem. They're a digestive Band-Aid, if you will. And all medications have side effects. If the root cause is not addressed, low immunity can eventually occur due to the improper assimilation of nutrients, which can open the door to viral and bacterial invaders.

At age fifty, poor digestion has many causative factors, such as eating too fast or, when stressed, eating too much; eating too many refined, acidic, fatty, and spicy foods; food sensitivities; allergies to wheat or dairy; poor diet with overconsumption of sugar; and poor elimination.

The most overlooked but vitally important factor is digestive enzyme deficiency. This is because we now live in a world where our foods are so microwaved, processed, nutrient poor, overcooked, and over-sugared that our own digestive enzymes—which are normally found in our digestive process—are often depleted by the enormous enzymatic workload they have to perform. Digestive enzymes are crucial for proper food assimilation.

It is at fifty that our enzyme bank account becomes low or overdrawn. This is when enzyme supplementation is not only important but necessary. According to DicQie Fuller, "Anytime we suffer from an acute or chronic illness, it is almost certain an enzyme-depletion problem exists."[1]

Enzymes are indeed crucial. Proponents of natural medicine refer to them as "little sparks of life." They turn all of the foods we ingest into energy and unlock this energy for use in the body. Enzymes have far-reaching benefits. They deliver nutrients, carry away toxic wastes, digest food, purify the blood, deliver hormones by feeding and fortifying the endocrine system, balance cholesterol and triglyceride levels, feed the brain, and, *most of all*, cause no harm to the body.

While it is possible to receive enzymes from raw foods that we eat, I strongly recommend that you make sure that you are "enzymatically insured" by supplementing your body with digestive enzymes from a plant source. Our busy lifestyles and hectic schedules have literally forced us to kill off the enzyme activity of our foods every time we microwave them. While it is true that we may occasionally eat foods that are packed with enzyme activity, our consumption of enzymatically dead or depleted food is greater.

Although mainstream medicine does not often recommend digestive enzymes to patients with digestive disturbances, many physicians have heard less from their patients once digestion is normalized by enzyme supplementation. Natural health practitioners believe that the first order of business when it comes to alleviating digestive discomfort and restoring the health of the digestive tract is to supplement with digestive enzymes. The "pink stuff" is just a cover-up!

Once you begin to supplement with enzymes, you will begin to notice several results. Some will be subtle; others will be dramatic. You will find that your energy increases, your sleep improves, and bloating and gas become a thing of the past. You may begin to lose that "spare midlife Michelin" around your waist. That heavy feeling after a meal will be gone, and instead it will be replaced with a lighter, more comfortable feeling. This is simply because the digestive tract, once freshly supplied with enzymes, will work like the well-oiled machine it was designed to be. No extra energy will be expended by the body on the digestive process because the enzymes will have lightened the workload.

Remember, food is fuel. It should energize you, not sideline you with fatigue and bloating. We are only as healthy as what we assimilate and eliminate. Enzymes help you do both. You can see the importance of enzymes in the restoration of proper digestion and, ultimately, health at age fifty.

GASTROINTESTINAL DEFENDERS

If you are battling any kind of digestive or intestinal problem, probiotics are a must. These gastrointestinal defenders are crucial in keeping your immune defense in good working order.

Probiotics consist mainly of *lactobacillus acidophilus* and *lactobacillus bifidus*. These produce volatile fatty acids, which provide metabolic energy. In addition, they help you digest food and amino acids, help you produce certain vitamins, and (most importantly) make your lower intestine mildly acidic, which inhibits the growth of bad bacteria such as E. coli, something that has caused serious illnesses in recent years.

Enzyme supplementation offers help for another midlife concern—antiaging. Younger-looking skin is an additional benefit enjoyed by regular enzyme use. This is because enzymes can increase the blood supply to the skin by delivering life-giving nutrients and carrying away waste products that can make your skin look tired and wrinkled. Because circulation slows down as we age, enzyme supplementation becomes crucial, not only for our outward appearance, but internally as well.

You can receive digestive enzymes through dietary supplements. A basic plant enzyme formula should contain the following:

- Amylase—digests carbohydrates

- Lipase—digests fats

- Protease—digests proteins

- Lactase—digests lactose (milk or sugar), our most common deficiency

Look for a plant enzyme formula containing these basic enzymes. In addition, look for a product that reports the enzyme product levels in FCC units. This will assure you of the active potent enzyme activity. I recommend you take enzymes at the beginning of each meal. This is when they have the highest effectiveness.

FIGHTING YEAST AND FUNGAL INFECTIONS

Another case in which it is absolutely essential to supplement with probiotics is in your fight against any midlife yeast or fungal infection. Probiotics possess antifungal properties.

According to Dr. James F. Balch in his best-selling book *Prescription for Nutritional Healing*, the flora in a healthy colon should consist of at least 85 percent lactobacilli and 15 percent coliform bacteria. The typical colon bacteria count today is the reverse, which has resulted in gas, bloating, intestinal and systemic toxicity, constipation, and malabsorption of nutrients, making it a perfect environment for the overgrowth of candida.

By adding probiotics (*lactobacillus acidophilus* and *lactobacillus bifidus*) supplements to your system, you will return your intestinal flora to a healthier balance and eliminate all of the problems of intestinal flora imbalance.

If you are taking antibiotics, it is especially important that you supplement your digestive tract with probiotics or "good bacteria," because antibiotics destroy your healthy bowel flora along with the harmful bacteria. Both *lactobacillus acidophilus* and *lactobacillus bifidus* promote proper digestion, help to normalize bowel function, and prevent gas and candida overgrowth. This in turn keeps midlife immunity high.

Store your probiotic formula in a cool, dry place. Some brands require refrigeration.

Enzyme supplementation, especially at age fifty, will put you in a more favorable position to fight biological and system malfunctions, while at the same time boosting your immune system. Enzyme therapy is another component of your age-defying preventative health arsenal. If you don't make them, take them!

Chapter 11

MIDLIFE PAINS—ARTHRITIS

Stress, strain, sore muscles, and pain. At fifty, osteoarthritis affects over 35 million Americans. Weight gain increases the risk of arthritic knees and hips. As a matter of fact, middle-aged women who lost eleven pounds over a ten-year period halved their risk of osteo-arthritic knees.

Yes, being fifty can literally be a pain. As baby boomers enter middle age and beyond, many of them struggle with mild to intense physical agony caused by bone degeneration. Whether this degeneration is due to swelling of the tissues that line the joints, to muscle strain, or to fatigue, the joints, muscles, bones, and tendons break down too soon for one out of every four American midlifers. In addition, these excru-ciating joint problems can lead to changes in both body and mind, which ultimately affect the spirit. This further intensifies the pain.

Stress can cause muscles to tense. Tense muscles can also occur in reaction to soreness in an affected area. This results in even more sen-sitive muscles. When joints deteriorate to the point of "bone on bone," nerves that register pain can actually grow and connect to other types of nerves. This can result in pain in areas nowhere near the original problem site. As pain continues, people often assume odd postures in order to avoid or lessen their discomfort, but this only results in straining other muscles. And unused muscles lose strength, which can cause additional discomfort.

Joint problems cause mental stress as well, which increases the release of adrenaline. Ultimately, this exhausts the body and mind. Depression occurs after the exhaustion phase, which again magnifies the discomfort. Serotonin levels drop as the action of the "feel good" brain chemicals are hindered. Sleep is disrupted by the pain, tension, and exhaustion, further inhibiting the body's ability to release natural mood elevators known as endorphins.

In an effort to break the cycle of pain, many fifty-year-olds are reaching for over-the-counter or prescription medications at an alarming rate, trying to carry on with their many daily responsibilities. They spend billions of dollars on NSAIDS (nonsteroidal anti-inflammatory drugs), aspirin, acetaminophen, ibuprofen, and COX-2 inhibitors. Fifty-year-olds can be too busy, too stressed, and too tired to actively take part in taking care of their joints, muscles, and compensatory postures. They believe that they have to just live with this "inevitable" part of midlife. A friend recently told me that these days his back went out more than he did!

At fifty, is it possible to find relief from the pain and suffering that affect your body and mind without taking these medications that have risks and side effects, such as liver and kidney damage, gastrointestinal bleeding, and even death? Absolutely! But you must become an active participant in your own recovery. Some nutritional approaches are highly effective, as you will soon learn.

NATURAL THERAPIES

There is hope that natural substances will someday soon revolutionize the treatment and management of arthritic disease. They may even help the body rebuild functioning joints.

Willow bark is rich in salicin and salicylates that metabolize into salicylic acid. Salicylic acid, the base of aspirin, was first prepared from willow bark in the late 1930s. Willow bark has fewer side effects than aspirin and has a long tradition of use in Europe. It has a pro-inflammatory effect. Fish oil helps to regulate inflammation. Omega-3 oils (EPA and DHA) and flax oil suppress inflammation especially well in rheumatoid arthritis (RA) patients.[1]

A one-year study revealed a significant anti-inflammatory effect when seventy-eight patients with an inflammatory disease were treated with an enteric fish oil preparation. At the end of the year, 59 percent of the treated group remained in remission, compared to 38 percent of the placebo group.[2]

Publications from around the world now confirm that omega-3 oils are effective in relieving morning stiffness and the tender joints associated with RA. Most promising of all is that in some instances omega-3 oil actually eliminated the need for NSAID medications.[3] Further, fish oil and low-dose aspirin, taken together, have been found to have better effects on inflammation than with either substance alone.[4]

Chrondroitin sulfate is a major component of cartilage and reduces pain while increasing range of motion with long-term use. Glucosamine alone or in combination with chondroitin sulfate is becoming the treatment of choice for osteoarthritis (OA). It has the ability to repair and improve joint function in addition to providing pain relief. Most of all, it offers no dangerous side effects.

Vitamin E is a powerful antioxidant that has been reported to diminish pain. Free-radical damage is a factor in the development of OA and RA patients. GLA (gamma-linolenic acid) is a fatty acid that has been used to suppress chronic inflammation. Dietary sources include black walnut seed oil, evening primrose oil, and borage oil. Nettle leaf has a long history of use as a safe remedy for arthritis in Germany. It is a natural COX-2 inhibitor, which means it suppresses the pro-inflammatory enzyme known as Cyclooxygenase-2, or COX-2.

Ginger root (not to be confused with *wild ginger*, which can be hazardous) is a powerful herb that possesses anti-inflammatory and antioxidant properties. It has been used for thousands of years for medicinal purposes in China for rheumatism, stomach distress, and nausea.

Natural therapies can be effective for the pain that comes with arthritis. They should be tried first, in my opinion, because they can provide relief from pain and inflammation without the negative side effects common to NSAID medications.

MASSAGE

Since massage improves circulation throughout the body, relieves headaches, and aids digestive disorders, fatigue, and much more, it is extremely therapeutic. It makes sense that there is a huge demand these days for therapeutic massage. Fifty-year-olds are driving this demand and are reaping great benefit. Massage aids in relaxation, gives relief from pain, and improves range of motion. In addition, it helps to release stored physical and emotional tension.

At age fifty, stress reduction and relaxation are the two things that people desperately need. Massage is a superior modality that has been used for thousands of years to relieve pain and stress. Like the millions of fifty-year-olds who came before us, we too can reap all of the same benefits! It is wise to make massage a part of your antiaging protocol.

Chapter 12

CANCER

Just hearing the word *cancer* seems to spark fear in the average person. By age fifty, virtually all of us have been touched somehow by this dreaded disease. Although the number of cancer cases is increasing, the good news is that there is also a rising group of cancer survivors. This is because our knowledge of the disease has changed. Early detection has always been one factor in survival and proper treatment.

We now know that most cancers respond positively to diet improvement. You can help your body rebuild healthy cells while starving out cancer cells by avoiding dead, demineralized, heavily processed foods; refined sugars; excessive caffeine; food dyes; and pesticide-sprayed foods, which cancer cells thrive on. Diet improvement will boost the immune system.

You must create an environment in your body in which cancer cannot flourish. Cancer attacks when the immune response is low, whether from overwork, emotional upheaval, poor diet, or exposure to toxic substances. All of these factors change your body chemistry in a negative way, making it hard for your immune system to defend you from disease. Knowledge is the key.

First, know the early detection signs. (Note that there are many possible causes for these symptoms; if you have one or more of them, it does not necessarily signal cancer.)

- Change in bowel or bladder habits, especially blood in the stool

- Chronic indigestion, bloating and heartburn, difficulty swallowing

- Unusual bleeding or discharge from the vagina

- Lump or thickening in the breast or testicles

- Chronic cough or constant hoarseness; bloody sputum (saliva)

- Changes or growth in warts or moles; dry, scaly skin patches that never heal, especially if they ulcerate or are inflamed

- Unusual weight loss

CUT YOUR RISK

- Two pieces of fruit and three vegetables a day show promising anticancer results. (In this case, more is better!)

- Reduce animal fat intake. (Toxins and pesticides are stored in animal fat.)

- Limit red meat intake.

- Boost your immune system. (Follow the plan in my book *90-Day Immune System Makeover*.)

- Detoxify your body twice a year (in the spring and fall) by using a natural, herbal cleansing product, such as those available at most health food stores.

- Take enzymes daily (to digest, assimilate, and eliminate properly).

- Drink plenty of water (eight to ten glasses per day).

- If you are on hormone therapy, use the lowest dose. Have your health care provider routinely check your blood or saliva levels to ensure proper dosage.

CANCER PREVENTION CHECKLIST[1]

- Cervical: Women who are eighteen and older (or whenever sexual activity begins) should have a Pap test done every year until age thirty-nine. Women who are forty and older should have a Pap test done every other year and a pelvic exam every year.

- Uterine/ovarian: Women eighteen to thirty-nine years of age should follow the above recommendations for a Pap test. Women forty years old and older should have a pelvic exam done every year. If there is a family history of ovarian cancer, you should also receive an annual CA 125 test.

- Rectal/prostate: Men and women forty years of age and older should have a digital rectal exam every year, and men fifty and older should have a prostate specific antigen (PSA) test every year.

- Colorectal: Men and women who are fifty and older should have a sigmoidoscopy (a test that uses a scope to inspect the sigmoid colon to detect polyps or other abnormalities that can become cancerous) every three to five years and a fecal occult blood test every year.

HEALTH UPDATE

Several studies have indicated that women who use talcum powder in the vaginal area after bathing have a 60 percent increased risk of ovarian cancer. Women using genital powder deodorant sprays have a 90 percent increased risk.[2] Avoid these products!

Chapter 13

DEPRESSION

By age fifty, many people may battle depression. If you are one of them, be encouraged: there is hope and help for you.

The underlying origins of depression are usually bottled-up anger or aggression turned inward, great emotional loss, and the inability to express grief. Depression can also be the result of negative emotional behavior, often learned in childhood, in an attempt to control relationships. Some cases of depression are drug-induced because prescription drugs can create nutrient deficiencies.

Depression can also be a result of prolonged stress, which causes a deficiency of amino acids, resulting in a biochemical imbalance. Other nutritional deficiencies, nervous tension, poor diet, mononucleosis, thyroid disorders, allergies, and serious physical disorders can also cause depression.

When certain nutrients are not supplied to the brain, a set of negative emotions can occur that affects our ability to cope with stressful situations that we confront during the fifth decade of life. Nutrition is crucial in the treatment of depression and key to your brain's behavior.

The many and varied symptoms of depression may include:

- Profound, persistent sadness

- Profound, persistent irritability

- Unexplained crying

- Loss of self-esteem

- Feelings of hopelessness

- Feelings of pessimism

- Feelings of helplessness

- Feelings of worthlessness

- Feelings of guilt

- Feelings of emptiness

- Continual mulling over the past, reviewing errors you have made

- Changes in sleeping patterns

- Changes in eating habits

- Unexplained weight gain or loss

- Restlessness

- Fatigue

- A "slow down" of physical movements

- Inability to concentrate

- Memory difficulties

- Difficulty making decisions

- Loss of interest in usually pleasurable activities

- Loss of interest in sex

- Unexplained headaches, upset stomach, or other physical problems that are not helped with standard treatment

- Thoughts of suicide or death

- Actual suicide attempts

There are different degrees of depression ranging from mild to severe. Treatments can range from electroconvulsant therapy (ECT) to therapy, drugs, and nutritional and lifestyle modification. Medications have helped many midlifers regain their sense of equilibrium, but these medications carry potentially serious side effects. Their use must be carefully monitored. Furthermore, studies have shown that drugs are of little or no value for 33 percent of depression sufferers. In an additional 33 percent of the cases, the medications were found to be little more effective than placebos.

The following are natural alternatives to the medication maze. Discuss these recommendations with your health care provider should you suspect that you are dealing with midlife depression.

YOUR PROTOCOL FOR DEALING WITH DEPRESSION

⭐ *Starred supplement: SAMe*

SAMe is one of the safest and most effective antidepressants in the world. When compared to other antidepressants, SAMe worked faster and more effectively with virtually no side effects.[1] SAMe produces side benefits as well, including improved cognitive function, liver function, and a potential slowing of the aging process. As a matter of fact, some people take SAMe for its antiaging properties alone.

Note: Refrigeration is recommended. Do not take with SSRI medications. For best results with SAMe, also take folic acid and vitamins B_{12} and B_6.

> **SAMe**
>
> Form: Capsule
>
> Dosage: 1,200–1,600 mg daily; take individual doses with food in the morning, midday, and late afternoon
>
> Frequency: Three times daily, with meals

⭐ Starred supplement: 5-HTP

5-HTP is an intermediate in the natural synthesis of the essential amino acid tryptophan to serotonin. 5-HTP encourages brain serotonin levels that can lead to positive effects on emotional well-being.[2]

Warning: Do not use 5-HTP with SSRI medications.

Second tier

It has been theorized that the following supplements may have beneficial effects for this condition of midlife:

- DHEA (dehydroepiandrosterone)—a hormone produced in the ovaries and glands of men and women. Though DHEA is important for good brain function, levels decline at midlife. DHEA relieves depression by improving psychological well-being. It may enhance memory, strengthen immunity, improve general physical condition, and make it easier to handle stress.[3]

- Pregnenolone—a hormone produced by the ovaries and the adrenal glands. Depressed people have less than normal amounts of pregnenolone in their spinal fluid. It may increase the ability to handle stress, have a beneficial effect on the brain and nervous system, and improve the ability to retrieve and remember information.

- L-carnitine—an amino acid that has been reported to safely alleviate depression in some people. It may also possess cognitive-enhancing, antiaging effects. Dosage: 1,000 mg twice daily.

- St. John's wort (hypericum)—an affordable herb that has been used for centuries to treat depression. This herb is used in Germany, where it is actually covered by health insurance. Noticeable results occur in about one month. Dosage: 300 mg three times daily. Please note that St. John's wort is not recommended for people who are taking MAO inhibitors. Note also that St. John's wort may interfere with other medications, including cancer medications. Consult your physician before using.

VITAMINS AND MINERALS FOR DEPRESSION

The following vitamins and minerals may be helpful in combating depression:

- Choline—this B-family vitamin may help push other B vitamins to the brain.

- Vitamin B_1—deficiency may lead to depression.

- Folic acid—low amounts of this member of the vitamin B family may be linked to depression.

- Vitamin B_2—proper levels may be linked to happiness.

- Vitamin B_3—deficiency may lead to worry, depression, and fear.

- Vitamin B_5—proper levels may lighten depression.

- Vitamin B_6—this B vitamin may help to quell emotional symptoms, especially in women. A link between vitamin B_6 deficiency and depression has been suggested.

- Vitamin B_{12}—deficiency may cause depression and confusion.

- Vitamin C—deficiency may lead to mental confusion and depression. Dosage: 1,000 mg twice daily.

- Potassium—low levels may be associated with mood upsets, fatigue, and weakness, which are all symptoms of depression. Dietary sources of potassium include bananas, oranges, peas, and nonfat milk.

- Fish oil (omega-3 fatty acids)—researchers have suggested that fish oils may lessen the symptoms of depression as well as other midlife diseases, such as arthritis and heart disease.

Look for a good B-complex multivitamin that contains the full spectrum of B vitamins with folic acid and choline. This may help prevent deficiency.

If you are experiencing signs of depression, you should immediately *avoid* alcohol, caffeine, and sugar, all of which cause changes in energy and mood.

Depression, once identified, can be treated and overcome. Fortunately, we are living in a time when several modalities are at our disposal to help us overcome this condition. Many people have developed their spiritual lives while walking through the dark valley of depression, emerging wiser and more grounded than ever before.

For more information, please contact the Depression and Bipolar Support Alliance at 1-800-826-3632.

Chapter 14

HEALTH SCREENINGS FOR WOMEN

When it comes to your health care, you may have the impression that age fifty marks the beginning of declining health. If you have never had a mammogram, your doctor will urge you to schedule one now. If you have neglected your vision, an eye exam will suddenly achieve priority status. Depending on your risk factors, your bone health may be evaluated. And on and on. Why is it vitally important to have all these tests when you hit fifty?

The fact is that prevention and early detection of disease should be the cornerstone of your age fifty wellness plan. Think of it as a personal health care evolution that began with the very first vaccine you received as a newborn.

Here is a list of the tests you should begin receiving when you turn fifty:[1]

- *Clinical skin exam.* Your doctor will do a head-to-toe skin check looking for irregular moles and other possible signs of skin cancer; women age fifty and older should have this test done once a year.

- *Colorectal cancer screenings.* Starting at age fifty, all adults should have a fecal occult blood test performed annually and a sigmoidoscopy every three to ten years to check for polyps or cancerous lesions; if you are at high risk for colorectal cancer, your physician may suggest a colonoscopy instead.

- *Total thyroxin test (T4).* This blood test assesses thyroid function; talk to your physician about getting the test done around menopause.

- *Bone density test.* You will need a baseline test at menopause to detect osteoporosis or assess your risk for the disease in the near future.

- *Clinical breast exam.* Your physician should examine your breasts each year to look for lumps, swollen lymph nodes, and other irregularities.

- *Mammogram.* A baseline mammogram is recommended by age forty, followed by mammograms every two years and annually after age fifty.

- *Pap smear.* You should have this test at least once every three years and annually if you are at high risk for cervical cancer. Yes, you need a Pap smear even if you have had a hysterectomy or are postmenopausal.

- *Glaucoma screening.* Get this eye test beginning at age forty. If you have normal vision, you should get an eye exam every three to five years.

- *Electrocardiogram (ECG).* You should get a baseline ECG by age forty. This painless test uses electrodes to record your heart's electrical impulses, and it evaluates heart function; it can identify injury or abnormality.

- *Blood pressure screening.* Your blood pressure should be checked at least once every two years. If your blood pressure is elevated, steps should be taken to control it, and more frequent monitoring may be required.

- *Cholesterol test.* If your total cholesterol levels (including LDL, HDL, and triglyceride levels) fall within the desirable range, this simple blood test, which helps assess your risk of cardiovascular disease, should be performed every five years.

This list covers general screening guidelines. Of course, every woman's needs are unique, so discuss your screening status with your doctor. He or she may suggest additional tests or a different schedule.

Chapter 15

PERIMENOPAUSE

Perimenopause (or premenopause) occurs in women around the age of forty and continues until the early fifties, when the menstrual period becomes a thing of the past. Perimenopause signals the beginning of menopause.

During this stage of life, many women experience a decrease or even cessation in their progesterone production because of irregular ovarian cycling and ovarian aging. At the same time, estrogen levels may be excessively or moderately high, causing a troubling state of continual imbalance. This condition is now recognized as "estrogen dominance." And therein lies most of the midlife woman's complaints.

Fatigue, breast tenderness, foggy thinking, irritability, headaches, insomnia, decreased sex drive, anxiety, depression, allergy symptoms (including asthma), fat gain—especially around the middle—hair loss, mood swings, memory loss, water retention, bone loss, endometrial cancer, breast cancer, and slowed metabolism make up some of the symptoms women endure for years on end. These are the symptoms and conditions of perimenopause.

Hormonal imbalance has far-reaching effects on many tissues in the body, including the heart, brain, blood vessels, bones, uterus, and breasts. The key to a smooth perimenopause is bringing the levels of estrogen and progesterone back into balance. Once this is accomplished, women feel wonderful again, complete with vitality, alertness, and optimism. They become more sociable and nurturing— to themselves and others.

According to the late pioneer of progesterone therapy, John R. Lee, MD, "One of progesterone's most powerful and important roles in the body is to balance and oppose estrogen."[1] The following list of estrogen and progesterone effects will further drive home the importance of natural progesterone use at midlife and beyond.

ESTROGEN VS. PROGESTERONE	
Estrogen	Progesterone
Increases body fat	Helps use fat for energy
Increases salt and fluid retention	Acts as a natural diuretic
Increases risk of breast cancer	May help prevent breast cancer
Decreases sex drive	Restores sex drive
Causes headaches and depression	Acts as a natural antidepressant
Impairs blood sugar control	Normalizes blood sugar levels
Increases risk of endometrial cancer	May help prevent endometrial cancer
Reduces oxygen in all cells	Restores proper cell oxygen

The following guidelines for using progesterone cream are based upon a 2-ounce container containing 960 mg total. Some women notice results right away. Others may see positive changes in one to three months.

For best results, use progesterone cream between ovulation until the onset of menses. If you have symptoms prior to ovulation (for example, migraines or moodiness), you may want to begin using the cream earlier, until your period. You do not need progesterone during menstruation. However, if you experience cramps or other symptoms during menstruation, you may use the cream until the symptoms are alleviated.

GENERAL GUIDELINES

Below are some general guidelines for perimenopausal progesterone use for women who still have their ovaries and uterus:

- After ovulation (days 14–18 after onset of last period): Use a small amount of cream, no more than ¼ teaspoon, once daily.

- Days 18–23: Use ¼ teaspoon twice daily, gradually increasing to ½ teaspoon twice daily.

- Day 23 to start of period: Use ½ teaspoon twice daily.

Other guidelines

- Women without ovaries due to hysterectomy should apply ¼ to ½ teaspoon of progesterone cream twice daily for twenty-five days of the calendar month, with five to seven without it.

- If you have endometriosis, you should use the progesterone cream on days 8–26 of your cycle.

- If you have ovaries but no uterus, use ¼ to ½ teaspoon twice a day for three weeks out of the month.

- Premenopausal women who are menstruating but not ovulating should use ¼ to ½ teaspoon daily. Begin using it on days 10–12 of your cycle. Continue until your expected period, and then stop.

Areas of application include chest, inner arms, neck, face, palms, and even the soles of your feet if they are not calloused. Cycle through the places you apply the cream, changing them every day. Apply in the morning and again at bedtime.[2]

PERIMENOPAUSE PROTOCOL

- Vitamin C: 1,000 mg daily

- Chromium: 200–400 mcg daily (blood sugar balancer)

- Magnesium: 400–600 mg at bedtime

- Zinc: 15–30 mg daily

- Vanadyl sulfate: 5–10 mg daily (blood sugar balancer)

- Calcium: Bone and tooth builder

- Boron: 1–5 mg daily (maintenance of strong bones)

- Vitamin D: 100–400 IU daily (bone health)

- Vitamin E: 200–400 IU daily (antioxidant, protects the cardiovascular system)

- B complex: Stress fighter

Chapter 16

NEXT STOP: MENOPAUSE

You're fifty. You're gaining weight, your periods have stopped, you have been diagnosed with uterine fibroids, your breasts are sore and lumpy, your skin has changed and lacks that velvety texture, your sex drive has decreased, you're irritable, you're anxious, and you're maybe even depressed. You would do anything for a good night's sleep. It is the time to fasten your seatbelt, because the roller-coaster ride is about to begin: you have reached menopause!

A new body of evidence points to hormonal imbalance, particularly an excess of estrogen and a deficiency of progesterone at menopause, as the cause of this life-disrupting symptomology. At fifty, women's lives seem to be just as imbalanced as their hormones. They are out of touch with their bodies and their feelings. Many times they are out of touch socially as they try to balance work and family life. They do not nurture themselves, so they wind up tired, bewildered, anxious, and depressed.

Unfortunately, the current thinking is to treat this phase of life as a disease state rather than a normal passage that was, in years past, nurtured with herbs, reassurance, and time-tested wisdom from older women who had taken the journey before them. Today the symptoms are more intense because lifestyles have changed. Stress levels are relentlessly high, further driving hormone levels down.

The medical profession has stepped in to try to squash these symptoms that negatively affect a midlife woman's life. Doctors offer prescription medications that elevate mood and alter personality until the smoke clears. In addition, synthetic hormone replacement has been a standard of midlife menopausal care. In 2002, a landmark study called the Women's Health Initiative was halted abruptly when it was found that Prempro, a synthetic estrogen/progestin medication used in the study, actually *increased* a woman's risk of heart attack, stroke, and breast cancer. The study was aborted due to the possibility of endangering the lives of the women in the study.

For the first time in several decades, doctors and patients alike are rethinking midlife hormonal health. Research has now shown that estrogen, when taken in excess, is a dangerous cancer promoter. It also fuels endometrial growth (endometriosis); encourages fibroid growth; contributes to fibrocystic breasts; and causes weight gain, headaches, gallbladder problems, and heavier periods, just to name a few of the negatives.

Menopausal women today are at a crossroads. Do they take estrogen for the sometimes-debilitating pains of menopause—and risk hormone-related cancer later on—or do they suffer in silence as their bodies ache and rapidly age? Do they live in a hormone-deficient state and subject themselves to the possibility of acquiring the degenerative diseases that attack a body lacking proper balance?

The good news is that you don't have to suffer and fall victim to accelerated aging and degenerative health conditions.

You may choose a natural menopause and implement a program of vitamins, minerals, and herbs, or use bio-identical hormones. These are derived from plant sources, namely soy or wild yam, and are identical to the hormones your body normally produces.

YOUR PROTOCOL FOR NATURAL MENOPAUSE MANAGEMENT

⭐ *Starred supplement: Black cohosh*

Black cohosh is an herb that alleviates anxiety, hot flashes, night sweats, vaginal dryness and atrophy, depression, heart palpitations, headaches, and sleep disturbances.[1]

Note: Consult with your health care provider before taking natural estrogenic supplements like black cohosh if you are on conventional hormone replacement therapy (HRT).

Black cohosh

Form: Capsule

Dosage: 80–160 mg in divided doses

Frequency: Once daily

⭐ *Starred supplement: Progesterone cream*

Natural progesterone can balance the ratio of estrogen and progesterone in your body, thereby alleviating all of the symptoms of estrogen dominance. In addition, it helps to build bone and relieve anxiety. It may also protect against breast cancer.[2]

Natural Progesterone

Form: Topical cream

Dosage: ¼–½ tsp

Frequency: Twice daily for three weeks, then one week with no cream. Follow the instructions in the perimenopause chapter to determine dosage and frequency based on your particular situation (such as whether or not you have had a hysterectomy).

Second tier

It has been theorized that the following supplements may have beneficial effects for this condition of midlife:

- Flaxseed—helps keep the skin supple and vaginal tissues healthy; also helps the body produce prostaglandins (inflammation fighters)

- Vitamin E—may reduce the risk of heart attack and stroke with 400–1600 IU daily; is also a skin nutrient and mood balancer and relieves hot flashes. Check with your physician if you have hypertension, diabetes, or menstrual bleeding problems.

- Fiber—keeps the body regular. Women who are constipated have four times the risk of breast cancer than women who are not.

- Gamma oryzanol—derived from rice bran oil; a dose of 300 mg daily diminishes hot flashes, headaches, sleeplessness, and mood swings

Chapter 17

BREAST HEALTH/BREAST DISEASE

Once a midlife woman finds a suspicious breast lump, her natural reaction is fear. But here are the facts: the majority of breast lumps are not cancerous. Although all breast lumps need medical evaluation, you should take comfort in the fact that any breast lump you discover is probably one of many types of harmless lumps that occur in breast tissue.

The most common cause of breast lumps is fibrocystic breast disease, which is characterized by cysts and a thickening of the milk glands. Symptoms include lumpiness in the breast and tenderness that becomes more pronounced just before the menstrual cycle. This condition typically affects women between the ages of thirty and fifty because this is when there is a higher incidence of hormonal fluctuations and imbalances, primarily estrogen dominance, which seems to "feed" cysts or multiply their occurrence. As a rule, benign lumps are usually tender and moveable while cancerous lumps are usually painless and do not move freely.

There are four basic types of breast lumps:

1. Lipoma—a benign, painless tumor made up of fatty tissue. Usually considered harmless, it has the potential to become malignant.

2. Fibroadenoma—commonly found in women twenty years old and older. It is usually a rubbery, firm, and painless mass commonly found on the upper portion of the breast.

3. Cystosarcoma—a fast-growing benign tumor that grows in the connective tissue of the breast. In rare instances, it can become malignant.

4. Carcinoma of the breast—a dimpled area of skin can be seen directly over the lump; can also include a dark discharge from the nipple. Malignant breast lumps are usually the size of a pea and are hard to the touch. In 90 percent of cases, only one breast is affected at a time.

Diagnostic methods include:

- Mammography

- Needle aspiration

- Ultrasound

- Thermographic screening

- Surgical biopsy

CHANGES IN YOUR DIET THAT MAY REDUCE YOUR RISK OF BREAST CANCER

- Limit coffee, tea, caffeine (directly linked to fibrocystic disease), and alcohol.

- Eat more cruciferous vegetables (such as broccoli, cabbage, and brussels sprouts) because they contain indoles, which help to protect breast tissue from estrogen metabolites.

- Eat a diet low in fat and high in fiber, whole grains, garlic, onions, fresh fruits, yogurt, and legumes.

- Focus on soy foods, which help to bind up bad estrogen.

- Limit or avoid animal and dairy products.

- Limit sugar, fried foods, white flour, and refined and processed foods.

YOUR PROTOCOL FOR REDUCING THE RISK OF BREAST CANCER

⭐ *Starred supplement: Natural progesterone cream*

Some clinical studies have suggested that progesterone cream may help prevent breast cancer. One study showed that the incidence of breast cancer was 5.4 times greater in women with low progesterone levels,[1] a finding that suggests adding progesterone back might help prevent breast cancer. Another study found further evidence suggesting the protective effects of progesterone cream on breast tissue.[2] Yet another study found that progesterone decreased cancerous cell proliferation by more than 400 percent.[3]

Natural Progesterone

Form: Topical cream

Dosage: ¼–½ tsp

Frequency: Follow the instructions in the peri-menopause chapter to determine dosage and frequency based on your particular situation (such as whether or not you have had a hysterectomy).

⭐ Starred supplement: Indole-3-carbinol

Indoles are phytochemicals (substances derived from plants) that may negate the effects of circulating bad estrogen to prevent further growth of breast tumors.[4]

Indole-3-carbinol (I3C), which is derived from cruciferous vegetables, may inhibit estrogen metabolites that are associated with breast and endometrial cancer. It is a powerful antioxidant that protects DNA and makes cells resistant to damage. Studies have shown that this vegetable extract may stop human cancer cells from growing by 54–61 percent and may even provoke cancerous cells to self-destruct (a phenomenon known as *apoptosis*). I3C also protects against dioxin, an environmental carcinogen.

For breast cancer health, I3C works to help modulate estrogen metabolism. In addition, it increases the conversion of estradiol to the weaker estrogen, with a 50 percent reduction within one week. Under laboratory conditions, it inhibited the growth of MCF7 breast cancer cells better than tamoxifen. I3C is activated by stomach acid, so do not take it with antacids.

Indole-3-Carbinol

Form: Capsule
Dosage: 200 mg
Frequency: Twice daily

Second tier

It has been theorized that the following supplements may have beneficial effects for this condition of midlife:

- Isoflavones—soy-based foods or capsules that may help protect breasts from tumor formation

- Evening primrose oil—an essential fatty acid thought to reduce breast lumps (because of its anti-prostaglandin agents)[5]

- Vitamin E—an antioxidant and hormone modulator. Studies have found that vitamin E dramatically decreases breast tenderness. Dosage: 800–1,200 IU daily.

- Vitamin A—reduces breast pain and is a free-radical scavenger. Helps breast ducts function optimally. Dosage: 10,000–15,000 IU daily.[6]

- Kelp—rich source of iodine. Breast disease is thought to be associated with iodine deficiency. Dosage: 1,000–2,000 IU daily.

- Water and fiber—aids digestion and bowel function. Women who are often constipated are four times more likely to develop breast cancer.

Additional therapy for breast health

- Apply hot moist packs on breasts.

- Apply warm castor oil packs.

- Manage stress with regular massage.

Chapter 18

LOVING THE SKIN YOU'RE IN

The skin care industry has become one of the largest, most profitable industries in America. Once again, this is largely due to baby boomers who are on a constant search for the latest and greatest botanical, liposomal, antioxidant, exfoliant, or hydrator in the world to make their midlife skin feel and appear visibly younger and smoother.

The fact is that beautiful skin is so much more than skin deep. Yes, there are the "lunchtime peels," microdermabrasion, laser resurfacing, and other techniques to smooth and erase fine lines, but it is an undeniable fact that beautiful skin is the result of a healthy, toxin-free, balanced body.

There are many factors that come into play in regard to great skin at fifty. Why is it that some women can go to the corner drugstore and use any moisturizer that may be on sale that week and have wonderful skin, complete with luminosity, velvety texture, and perfect tone, while others travel to major department stores to purchase only the highest-quality skin care products (with a price tag to match) and yet are still dissatisfied with their complexion?

The answer is simple in one sense, but complex in terms of all of the systems of the body that play a role in beautiful skin. The skin is the largest organ of the body. It receives great benefit from an enzyme-rich circulatory system. Skin that is well enriched by oxygen and high-quality nutrients will always look smooth, firm, and velvety.

Enzymes are the digestive catalysts that make nutrients available to the blood for their journey to every cell in the body. To feed your cells, detoxify your system, slow the aging process, oxygenate, and boost your circulatory system, you must make midlife enzyme supplementation a priority. Your skin needs constant and continuous nutrition from within that only enzymes can supply. Many notice that long-standing skin conditions begin to clear up after just fourteen days of enzyme therapy.

The goal is to take digestive enzymes from a plant source with each meal. The formula of your supplement should contain the following: amylase, lipase, protease, cellulase, lactase, maltase, and sucrase. Take this with meals. Between meals, to detoxify and fortify your system, take protease—330,000 to 420,000 HUT, as recommended by DicQie Fuller in her book *The Healing Power of Enzymes*. Protease is the most important enzyme for healthy skin.

MIDLIFE SKIN-BEAUTIFYING ENZYMES

- Protease—breaks down protein foods that feed the cells of the dermis; also improves distribution of all nutrients to the skin

- Amylase—reduces skin inflammation

- Lipase—keeps skin cells plump to reduce wrinkling

- Cellulase—breaks down fiber and allows nutrients access to the skin

SKIN SO SOFT

When we were young, our skin was soft, supple, and glowing. Beautiful skin came naturally in our youth. But as we have aged, beautiful skin has become a reward for taking proper care of our bodies. The skin is a barometer that reveals what is going on with us internally.

Skin care is big business these days as those of us fifty and over anxiously take part in staving off the signs of aging. Stress, excessive sun exposure, liver malfunction, hormone depletion, smoking, alcohol, sugar, fried foods, caffeine, and poor circulation all contribute to the condition of our skin. Age spots, wrinkles, dry skin, uneven skin tone, sallow complexion, and acne are the result of how well our systems handle wastes. Free-radical damage is another major contributor to poor skin.

Dietary therapy

- Drink plenty of water (six to eight glasses each day).

- Add fresh lemon to your water for added benefit.

- Make a fresh "liver cocktail" each day: 2 ounces beet juice, 3 ounces carrot juice, and 3 ounces cucumber juice (use a juicer).

- Avoid sugars, caffeine, and red meat to prevent dehydration.

- Eat fresh fruits and vegetables each day; fruits are wonderful cleaners.

Herbal and natural remedies

- Whole-body herbal cleansing formula

- Ginkgo biloba—increases circulation

- ACES—vitamins A, C, and E, and selenium—for free-radical damage

- Coenzyme Q_{10}—100 mg daily

- Evening primrose oil

- Dr. Janet's Woman's Balance Progesterone Formula— available at www.DrJanetPhD.com

- Alpha-hydroxy acids (fruit acid)—to exfoliate the skin

Body therapy

- Reduce or prevent wrinkles by rubbing papaya skins on the face. (Papain is an enzyme that exfoliates the skin.)

- Manage stress.

- Practice deep breathing.

- Have a massage with almond oil, sesame oil, or wheat germ oil to soften the skin.

- Moisturize immediately after bathing.

- Rub lemon juice on age spots or use 2 percent hydro-quinone topical cream to reduce and fade age spots.

- Limit sun exposure; always use a sunblock of SPF-15 or higher to prevent further damage and to prevent age spots from darkening.

Beauty big three

1. Detoxify and eat healthily.

2. Moisturize and drink plenty of water.

3. Protect by using sunscreen and limiting sun exposure.

HEALTH UPDATE

Watermelon juice is rich in natural silica, which supports collagen and reduces wrinkled and dry skin. The condition of your skin can be the first thing to alert you that you need to start a detoxification program. If your colon becomes stagnant with toxins and your liver does not filter wastes and impurities coming from the digestive tract, your skin will give you a sure sign—rashes, acne, boils, blotchiness, uneven skin tone, dermatitis, and itchy skin. After detoxification, your skin will glow and your skin problems will diminish or disappear.

Chapter 19

GOTTA GO RIGHT NOW!— URINARY TRACT HEALTH

Women who are going through premenopause/menopause have an increased risk of urinary tract infections. This is most likely due to changing ratios of estrogen and progesterone. A reduced level of estrogen in a midlife woman's system tends to enhance the adhesive qualities of the bladder's lining, thereby preventing proper bacterial removal upon urination.

In addition, by the time a woman reaches fifty, the muscles of the pelvic floor are weakened as the result of previous pregnancies and deliveries. This can cause the bladder to sag, which in turn contributes to the growth of bacterial colonies. Aging, poor posture, spinal disorders, excessive abdominal fat, and chronic constipation are other contributing factors.

Symptoms that may indicate a urinary tract infection include increased urination, a burning sensation while voiding, an intense need to urinate during the night, and a constant feeling of urgency or incomplete urination. A more serious infection involving the kidneys, which can develop if the infection is not tended to promptly, is characterized by blood in the urine, fever, chills, and nausea.

YOUR PROTOCOL FOR URINARY TRACT HEALTH

⭐ *Starred supplement: Cranberry*

Unsweetened cranberry juice or cranberry capsules may increase the acidity of the urine, which in one study significantly reduced the frequency of bacteria and pus in the urine of elderly women.[1]

Note: Purchase pure, unsweetened juice only, as commercial cranberry juice cocktail products contain high-fructose corn syrup.

> **Cranberry**
> Form: Juice (unsweetened) or capsule
> Dosage: Juice, 1 quart; capsule, 400 mg
> Frequency: Juice, 1 quart daily; capsule, one 400
>   mg capsule four times daily

Second tier

It has been theorized that the following supplements may have beneficial effects for this condition:

- Vitamin C—1,000 mg three times daily to acidify urine

- Antiseptic herbs—goldenseal, garlic, uva ursi

- Soothing demulcents—marshmallow root, corn silk

- Diuretic herbs—parsley

- Cucurbita pepo (commonly known as pumpkinseed extract)—support for healthy bladder and urinary function; promotes healthy bladder and urinary function in both men and women at midlife. In vitro studies show that pumpkinseed extract modulates aromatase, which converts testosterone to estradiol in women. A decrease in this conversion helps to maintain healthy testosterone levels in women, thus benefiting pelvic muscles and bladder function. Pumpkinseed extract has also been found to help postmenopausal women maintain healthy daytime and nighttime urination. Pumpkinseed extract has been well researched for promoting healthy urinary function in men by maintaining healthy levels of DHT for prostate and urinary health. This has led researchers to suggest that cucurbita pepo may promote healthy male and female urinary and bladder function.

Finally, you will also help your urinary tract by drinking eight glasses of water daily and by exercising.

Chapter 20

MALE MENOPAUSE—ANDROPAUSE

While everyone knows that women journey through menopause and all of its life-disrupting symptoms, men's bodies are experiencing hormonal changes as well. As testosterone production decreases, men feel less vital and less virile. They experience loss of muscle mass and strength, their energy declines, and their hairline recedes or disappears completely. For men, this lesser-known physiological change is known as andropause, or male menopause.

We are fast moving away from the term "male midlife crisis." It is now recognized that men fall victim to decreased hormonal levels at midlife just as their female counterparts do. It is a very real physiological condition. And it is very unsettling to most men. Men experiencing these midlife hormonal shifts may try desperately to regain or recapture their more youthful days. That, in itself, has led to many midlife marriage meltdowns.

Our society worships youth. Youthful images are splashed across magazine pages; television promotes reality shows featuring extreme makeovers—all of which leave us with one goal in mind: to turn back the clock. Men are not immune to these messages.

As a woman goes through the often-turbulent waters of menopause, she may be unresponsive sexually, fatigued, anxious, and depressed. She may experience bladder infections; fibroid tumors;

lengthy, irregular, and heavy menstrual cycles; bloating; and more. All of these conditions make romantic interludes impractical and unwelcome.

Women often feel less attractive during this time and tend to withdraw—and many men take it personally. They may take it as disinterest, which can amplify the feelings of inadequacy that men are dealing with at midlife. As a result, many men may seek the attentions of younger, more vibrant women during this time. In an effort to recapture youth, some midlife men have stepped out of their marriages into adulterous affairs. This has become so common that we often hear the phrase "midlife crisis" given as the acceptable, understandable reason for the indiscretion.

It has been estimated by some researchers that currently as many as 2.5 million American men between the ages of forty and fifty-five are experiencing signs and symptoms of andropause. Most of these physical, mental, and emotional changes take place over the course of ten to fifteen years. As a man reaches midlife, he may notice that his eight hours of uninterrupted sleep become a thing of the past as he makes his way to the bathroom in the middle of the night yet again due to increased urinary frequency. Abdominal fat now replaces a formerly well-toned stomach, and the hairline and libido start fading simultaneously.

The importance of testosterone cannot be stressed enough. It plays a vital role in a midlife male's sense of well-being. It has a positive effect on cholesterol levels, bone density, muscle mass, protein breakdown, and the maintenance of secondary sex characteristics, such as libido, facial and body hair, and more.

When it comes to measuring testosterone levels in midlife males, most mainstream labs have inadequate standard reference ranges—ranges that are well below optimal for midlife male rejuvenation. Therefore many men will have their blood drawn for testing and receive results that say their testosterone level is within the normal range for midlife males, when in fact their level is too low for midlife rejuvenation. The optimal testosterone level for aging males is the same as that of a healthy twenty-one- to thirty-one-year-old male.

A recent study revealed the effects of testosterone supplementation on ten men, ages sixty to seventy-eight, in a double-blind trial. The results were impressive. Testosterone supplementation improved exercise endurance time, increased fat-free mass (muscle), and improved balance.[1]

A very important fact for midlife men to note is that testosterone can be converted to different hormones by way of enzymatic pathways. One particular enzyme, called aromatase, which is found in the brain, fat, bone, and skin, can change testosterone into estrogen. Yes, men have estrogen, too. And estrogen has much benefit. However, excess estrogen (estradiol, in particular) has been linked to prostate cancer at midlife and beyond. Excess estrogen in both men and women at midlife appears to put both sexes at risk for hormone-related cancers.

When men are in their youth and their testosterone levels are at their peak, prostate cancer is virtually unheard of. It is only at midlife, when testosterone declines and estrogen levels are higher, that we hear about the very real threat of prostate cancer. A study conducted in 1994 on the effects of estrogen and testosterone on the prostate found that rats treated with testosterone alone showed less prostate growth than rats treated with both testosterone and estrogen.[2]

MEN AT MIDLIFE: RUNNING ON EMPTY

A midlife man produces 60 percent less testosterone than he did at age twenty.[3] If you are a man over forty years old, you are probably feeling the effects of low testosterone levels: depression, cognitive impairment, reduced sex drive, and abdominal weight gain. Low testosterone has been implicated as a major contributor to the development of heart disease in men.[4]

If you decide to try testosterone replacement therapy, remember that balance is the key. It is important to work with your physician.

The following guidelines should be observed when beginning testosterone replacement therapy.

- Step 1: Have a blood test done for PSA (prostate-specific antigen), liver function, estradiol (estrogen), DHEA, and testosterone. In addition, have a complete blood chemistry (CBC) done to access your general health.

- Step 2: If your estradiol level is elevated (over 30 pg/ml) and/or your testosterone level is low or low normal, you may want to have your physician prescribe a testosterone cream or gel like AndroGel. If your estrogen (estradiol) level is high, your doctor may want to prescribe an aromatase inhibitor, such as Arimidex, to inhibit the conversion of testosterone to estrogen. *Note*: While restoring free testosterone to healthy physiological levels (25–40 pg/ml) does not cause prostate cancer, it can induce existing prostate cancer cells to proliferate faster. Your physician can answer your questions on this matter.

- Step 3: You should have a digital rectal exam done before using testosterone, while also making sure that your PSA is well within the healthy range. While on testosterone therapy, you should have your blood drawn every six months to make sure your levels are in range. *Do not use testosterone replacement if you have prostate cancer.* Ask your physician about Arimidex, an aromatase inhibitor you should perhaps be taking while replacing testosterone.

SYMPTOMS OF LOW TESTOSTERONE

- Inability to concentrate
- Irritability

- Feeling weak

- Passive attitude

- General tiredness

- Diminished sex drive

- Memory failure

- Moodiness

- Anxiety

- Depression

TESTOSTERONE DRUGS

Here is a list of currently available natural testosterone drugs (consult your health care provider for more information):

- Testoderm TTS (Alza's testosterone patch)

- Androderm transdermal system (SmithKline Beecham's testosterone patch)

- Testosterone creams, pellets, and sublingual tablets (available from compounding pharmacies)

Both synthetic and natural testosterone drugs require a prescription—and a prescription should be written only after blood or saliva tests reveal a testosterone deficiency.

I recommend reading *The Testosterone Syndrome* by Eugene Shippen, MD.[5]

BOOST TESTOSTERONE NATURALLY

Since most aging men are testosterone deficient, boosting testosterone levels is an important part of a midlife male's health. It is the most important step you can take to regain your health and improve your performance.

A natural alternative to testosterone replacement therapy is a combination of chrysin (a flavonoid, or plant pigment, that blocks the aromatase enzyme that causes testosterone conversion to estrogen, thereby boosting levels of free testosterone naturally), muira puama, and urtica dioica (plant extracts that naturally reduce the conversion of testosterone to estrogen, effectively increasing free testosterone levels).[6] *Men with prostate cancer should avoid these ingredients.*

Muira puama dosage: 850 mg plant extract capsule one time daily. Urtica dioica dosage: 200 mg plant root capsule one time daily. Chrysin dosage: 1,500 mg capsule one time daily.

STEPS TO NATURALLY INHIBIT AROMATASE

- Reduce or eliminate alcohol to enable your liver to better remove excess estrogen.

- Make sure you are getting enough zinc (80–90 mg daily), since zinc functions as a natural aromatase inhibitor.

- Lose weight. Fat cells, especially in the abdominal area, produce the aromatase enzyme, which converts testosterone to estrogen.

THE RESEARCH

Here are some clinical studies that show the importance of restoring testosterone to youthful levels:

- By the time men reach age sixty, they produce 60 percent less testosterone than they did at age twenty. With this reduction come several well-documented disorders: depression, reduced sex drive, abdominal weight gain, and cognitive impairment.[7]

- Low testosterone has been suggested as a possible major cause in the development of heart disease.[8]

- Studies show that men who reestablish youthful levels of testosterone have the highest degree of protection against atherosclerosis, a leading cause of death of men worldwide.[9]

ARE HORMONAL IMBALANCES ENDANGERING YOUR HEALTH?

Hormones are life-sustaining chemical messengers that regulate human growth and development, sexual function, metabolism, and well-being. Unfortunately, blood levels of these critical hormones decline by age fifty.

While many mainstream doctors dismiss the importance of restoring youthful hormone levels in their fifty-plus-year-old patients, accepting diminished hormone status as an inevitable consequence of aging, research indicates that low hormone levels contribute to a vast array of debilitating conditions. By optimizing your hormone levels, you can help prevent many degenerative and debilitating conditions.

HORMONE TESTING IS ESSENTIAL TO EVERY ANTIAGING PROGRAM!

The following are samples of hormonal panels that can be ordered by your physician to determine if bioidentical hormone therapy (plant-sourced hormone therapy) is right for you.

Female hormone panel

- Pregnenolone

- DHEA-S

- Total Testosterone and Free Testosterone

- Progesterone

- Lipid Profile

- TSH

- Total Estrogens

Male hormone panel

- Pregnenolone

- DHEA-S

- Total Testosterone and Free Testosterone

- PSA

- Estradiol

- Progesterone

- Lipid Profile

- TSH

Chapter 21

PROSTATE HEALTH AT FIFTY

I t is quite common, even inevitable, that a man's prostate will enlarge as he ages. This is called BPH: benign prostatic hypertrophy or benign prostatic hyperplasia. The good news is that there are potent herbs that can be used to help alleviate discomfort while offering a level of protection against the formation of aberrant cells.

YOUR PROTOCOL FOR PROSTATE HEALTH

⭐ *Starred supplement: Pygeum*

Pygeum has been shown to alleviate prostate discomfort by inhibiting inflammatory processes.

> **Pygeum**
>
> Form: Soft gelcaps
> Dosage: 100 mg (divided into two doses)
> Frequency: 50 mg with breakfast, 50 mg with
> dinner

⭐ *Starred supplement: Saw palmetto*

Saw palmetto helps reduce urinary frequency and inflammatory action in the prostate gland. In addition, saw palmetto reduces smooth muscle contraction, which helps to relax the bladder and sphincter muscles that contribute to urinary frequency. Normal aging causes the ratio of testosterone to become imbalanced. It is important to inhibit the effects of estrogens, sex hormones, and DHT (dihydrotestosterone), and saw palmetto may help do this.[1]

Saw Palmetto

Form: Capsule

Dosage: 160 mg

Frequency: Twice daily with meals

Second tier

It has been theorized that the following supplements may have beneficial effects for this condition of midlife:

- Lycopene—studies have suggested a significant inverse relationship with the ingestion of lycopene-rich foods like tomatoes, tomato sauce, and pizza with the development of prostate cancer. A 41 percent reduction in prostate cancer was recorded in men who ingested ten or more servings of tomatoes in several forms per week. This was compared to men who ate four to seven servings, who reported only a 22 percent reduction.

- Nettle root extract—may help suppress the effects of estrogen by stopping it from binding to prostate cells[2]

- Indole-3-carbinol (or I3C)—may slow the propagation of aberrant prostate cells

- Zinc—a natural aromatase inhibitor. Dosage: 30–90 mg daily.

Chapter 22

YOUR EYESIGHT AND YOU

It happens almost overnight, or so it seems. You may be dining with friends, looking up a number in the phonebook, or reading a good book. Suddenly you realize your eyes are having more trouble focusing than they once did. You may find that you need to wear "cheaters," or magnifiers, to help you read with accuracy once again. No, your arms haven't gotten shorter; you are experiencing midlife ocular changes.

Eye exams are extremely important at midlife to safeguard you or treat any problem that may have developed.

Degenerative changes in the eye often begin in middle age, resulting in macular degeneration, glaucoma, cataracts, and other forms of retinopathy in later life. Our young eyes had high concentrations of natural antioxidants that protected us from cataract formation, macular degeneration, and other eye disorders. Older eyes fall prey to excessive free-radical damage and reduced circulation to the eye.

Antioxidant supplements have been shown to help protect against eye disorders.[1]

YOUR PROTOCOL FOR EYE HEALTH

✪ *Starred supplement: Bilberry*

Bilberry reduces visual fatigue and improves light-to-dark adjustment. It is a potent antioxidant that supports the integrity of vascular walls. Bilberry is a safe, natural way to enhance the function and strength of both the visual and vascular system.[2]

Bilberry

Form: Capsule

Dosage: 150 mg

Frequency: Once daily

✪ *Starred supplement: Lutein*

Lutein is a carotenoid that helps preserve eye health. It is found in dark green, leafy vegetables such as spinach, kale, collards, and broccoli. Lutein positively affects the health of the macular pigment to help prevent age-related macular degeneration (AMD).[3]

Lutein

Form: Capsules or soft gelcaps

Dosage: 10 mg

Frequency: Once daily

Second tier

It has been theorized that the following supplements may have beneficial effects for this condition of midlife:

- Vitamin A—an antioxidant that is especially good for retinal health; may decrease the risk of cataracts[4]

- Vitamin E—an antioxidant that has a protective effect against cataracts; protects against ultraviolet radiation exposure[5]

Chapter 23

WIRED BUT TIRED— ADRENAL EXHAUSTION

Around the time Jane turned fifty, she began noticing she was having a difficult time getting up in the morning. She experienced continuing fatigue that was not relieved by sleep. She also craved salty foods. She was lethargic; everything seemed like a chore. It took increased effort for her to accomplish everyday tasks.

Her list of complaints grew longer. Jane found she had a decreased ability to handle stress. Romantic interludes with her husband were not appealing at all because she barely had enough energy to keep going each day. The respiratory infection she caught in August was still hanging on in late September, and she found herself getting light-headed when she stood up quickly. It was hard for her to concentrate, and her memory was poor. This made her mildly depressed. During this time Jane also found that she had begun to feel better after dinner and during late evening hours. Her energy seemed to return at night.

Jane was suffering from the classic symptoms of low adrenal function. At midlife, an often-misunderstood, unrecognized, and underdiagnosed condition often smolders just below the surface. It is known as *hypoadrenia*, or adrenal exhaustion.

Weighing less than a cherry and no larger than a prune in size, your two adrenal glands sit perched atop your kidneys. From this vantage point, they greatly affect the function of every single tissue, gland, and organ in your body. In addition, they also have a profound effect on the way you think and feel. At midlife, your energy, your endurance, and your very life depend heavily on proper adrenal function. It is at midlife that 80 percent of Americans suffer from some degree of adrenal meltdown. There seems to be an epidemic of it due to excessive physical, emotional, and environmental stress.

Persons experiencing low adrenal function often experience the following symptoms: low blood pressure, fatigue, lethargy, changes in sex drive (usually low or nonexistent), electrolyte and fluid imbalance, and changes in fat metabolism and the heart and cardiovascular system. In addition, the body shape can change to more of an "apple" due to excess fat distribution in the midsection.

People with low adrenal function live with a feeling of general unwellness. They often turn to coffee, teas, colas, chocolate, and other stimulants to keep their energy levels up long enough to make it through the day. Unfortunately, these substances only tax the adrenals more, which in turn creates a vicious circle or merry-go-round that is hard to break out of.

Low blood sugar is also a part of the hypoadrenic picture, as well as allergies, asthma, low immunity, and arthritic pain. Midlife mental health is also affected by poor adrenal health. Symptoms include anxiety, depression, fearfulness, difficulty concentrating, confusion, and frustration. If the condition is ignored, hypoadrenia can lay the foundation for more serious health conditions, such as fibromyalgia, asthma, autoimmune disorders, diabetes, and respiratory infections.

Why is midlife the most common time for hypoadrenia to surface? The answer is simple: stress. Midlife, unlike any other period, often deals us stressful, life-changing events. We have experienced raising a family and all of the stress (good and bad) that goes along with it; we have built careers; we have strived for happy marriages and families; we may have had an operation or two; and we may have lost a job, a dear friend, a parent, or even the beloved family pet. We may have had a car accident, gone bankrupt, been divorced, had in-law problems, worked too much, and played too little. Most of all, we may not have taken the time to develop a close, personal relationship with our Creator.

Adrenal fatigue is usually triggered or caused by stress, whether it comes from a low-grade infection, physical stress, emotional turmoil, or psychological distress. Your adrenal glands are affected by every kind of stress. The adrenals are much like batteries that are drained each time a stressor affects our life. If these batteries are not recharged by resting enough, eating a proper diet, supplementing the body with adrenal-specific nutrients, and getting enough exercise, if you have not forgiven enough in your personal life, and if you continue to consume stimulants (caffeine, sodas, teas, and so forth), a meltdown is possible.

It is harder to rebuild your system after a meltdown occurs. Prevention is far and away the best route to take. Too many traumatic events and relentless stress will affect your adrenal glands' ability to recover. Over time, adrenal exhaustion may become the only state you know. People who suffer from this condition will often say, "I feel like I am just existing" or "I don't know where I went."

Certain personality traits and lifestyle factors are common to persons with low adrenal function. (Note that having one or more of these traits or factors does not necessarily mean you have hypoadrenia.) They are:

- Perfectionism

- Lack of sleep

- Being driven

- Using stimulants

- "Type-A" personalities

- Lack of leisure time and activities

- Keeping late hours

- Staying in no-win situations (which creates stress and frustration)

It is during midlife, when we are struggling just to keep up with daily demands, that the adrenals need to be strengthened and fortified. This is especially true for premenopausal/menopausal women. Around the age of fifty, the adrenals are designed to do "double duty" and pick up the slack for the ovaries as they begin to shut down their production of sex hormones. If the adrenals are taxed and worn out, they cannot help smooth out the transition into menopause.

This is why many "Type A" women experience an almost unbearable menopause, complete with severe anxiety, monster hot flashes, extreme fatigue, and more. These women are often prescribed Paxil, Xanax, and the like just to get them through these transitional years while at the same time sparing their families from dealing with "Mom and her emotional imbalances." The good news is that you can recover from this condition that robs many fifty-year-olds of vibrant health and joy.

EIGHT WARNING SIGNS OF ADRENAL EXHAUSTION

Some of the causes of hypoadrenia are unrelenting stress; Type-A personality; long-term use of cortico-steroid drugs for asthma, arthritis, and allergies; too much sugar and caffeine in the diet; the onset of menopause; and deficiency in vitamins B and C.

Let's look at some warning signs. (Note that having one or more of these symptoms does not necessarily mean you have hypoadrenia.) They include:

- Severe reactions to odors or certain foods

- Recurring yeast infections

- Heart palpitations and panic attacks

- Dry skin and peeling nails

- Clammy hands and soles of feet

- Low energy and poor memory

- Chronic low back pain

- Cravings for salt and sugar

SELF-TEST FOR ADRENAL EXHAUSTION

If you want to see just how well your adrenal glands are performing, try this self-test. You will need a blood pressure cuff and a place to lie down.

First, lie down and rest for five minutes. Then take your blood pressure (while still lying down). Stand up immediately and take your blood pressure reading once more. If your blood pressure is lower after you stand up, you probably have reduced adrenal gland function, which means your batteries need a charge.

The lower the second blood pressure reading is from your resting blood pressure, the more severely low your adrenal function may be. The systolic number (the number on top of the blood pressure reading) is normally about ten points higher when you are standing than when you are lying down. A difference of more than ten points should be addressed immediately, as it is of extreme importance in the journey back to health. Consult your physician.

YOUR PROTOCOL FOR ADRENAL HEALTH

✪ Starred supplement: Pantothenic acid

Pantothenic acid is a B vitamin known as an antistress vitamin. It may also play a role in the production of adrenal hormones. It is very helpful in alleviating anxiety and depression because it fortifies the adrenal glands. In addition, you need pantothenic acid to produce your own natural pain relievers, such as cortisol. This is very important because pain often goes hand-in-hand with emotional depletion.

Pantothenic Acid

Form: Capsule

Dosage: 100 mg

Frequency: Three times daily

⭐ Starred supplement: Vitamin C

Vitamin C is required for tissue growth and repair, healthy gums, and adrenal gland function. Vitamin C also protects against infection and strengthens immunity.[1]

Vitamin C

Form: Tablet or capsule

Dosage: 3,000–4,000 mg

Frequency: Daily (in divided doses)

⭐ Starred supplement: L-tyrosine

L-tyrosine is an amino acid that helps build the body's natural supply of adrenaline and thyroid hormones. It converts to L-dopa, which makes it a safe therapy for depression. L-tyrosine supports the production of catecholamine neurotransmitters, enhancing mood and cognitive function especially in situations involving stress or when dopamine, epinephrine, or norepinephrine levels require additional support.[2]

L-tyrosine has been used for stress reduction, anxiety, depression, and allergies. It also aids adrenal function.

Note: If you are on antidepressants or have cancer, you should avoid tyrosine.

L-tyrosine

Form: Capsule

Dosage: 500 mg

Frequency: Once daily (taken at bedtime or with a
high-carb meal so it does not have to compete
with other amino acids for absorption)

Second tier

It has been theorized that the following supplements may have beneficial effects for this condition:

- B complex—consists of the full spectrum of B vitamins, which help maintain a healthy nervous system. B complex comes in two standard doses: 50 and 100 mg. The 50 mg dosage is the recommended daily dosage for people who are already taking a multivitamin that has B vitamins in it.

- Royal jelly—is thought to be a blessing for the body against asthma, liver disease, skin disorders, and immune suppression. This is because it is rich in vitamins, minerals, enzymes, and hormones. In addition, it possesses antibiotic and antibacterial properties. It is interesting to note that it naturally contains a high concentration of pantothenic acid. Dosage: 2 teaspoonfuls daily.

- Astragalus—an herb that aids adrenal gland function. It also combats fatigue and protects the immune system. This herb played a large part in fortifying and strengthening my body when I battled the Epstein-Barr virus. It truly is a powerful herb in terms of immune boosting. Dosage: as directed on the bottle.

ADDITIONAL ADRENAL FORTIFIERS

- Rest, rest, rest!

- Brown rice, almonds, garlic, salmon, flounder, lentils, sunflower seeds, bran, brewer's yeast, and avocado

- Wheat germ

- Flaxseed

- Milk thistle

- Licorice root

- Hawthorn

- Gotu kola

- Siberian ginseng

- A daily green drink

Chapter 24

STOP AND SMELL THE ROSES—AROMATHERAPY

Aromatherapy is a safe, pleasant way to lift your mood and relieve stress. Smell is the most rapid of your five senses. Upon smelling something, the information is directly relayed to the hypothalamus, where your motivations, moods, emotions, and creativity all begin.

The aroma of essential oil molecules works through hormone-like chemicals to produce results. Scents and odors influence the glands responsible for hormone levels, metabolism, insulin, stress levels, appetite, body temperature, and even sex drive. Actual studies of brain waves show that scents like lavender increase alpha brain waves (associated with relaxation) and scents like jasmine boost beta waves (linked to alertness). Essential oils are most commonly used to counteract stress, which affects the mind and emotions. Essential oils used in aromatherapy can calm or uplift the body, mind, and spirit.

The effects of aromatherapy are immediate and profound on the central nervous system. In addition, aromatherapy makes you feel good by releasing mood-inducing neurochemicals in the brain. Aromatherapy promotes relaxation, alertness, restful sleep, and physical relaxation, and it can increase energy. It works by stimulating a release of neurotransmitters once an essential oil is inhaled. Neurotransmitters are brain chemicals responsible for pain reduction and pleasant feelings. Aromatherapy can also help prevent panic attacks. I personally can attest to this. You will be pleased to know that stress reduction is an aromatherapy specialty.

Listed below are essential oils that will help your body, mind, and spirit as you continue on your journey to making fifty the new thirty. They are wonderful healing tools.

AROMATHERAPY ESSENTIAL OILS

For Stress

Lavender—balances your nerves and emotions; calms the heart, thereby helping lower high blood pressure

Sandalwood—good for sleep and relaxation

Clary sage—promotes feelings of well-being, calms nerves, lifts the mood, and diminishes stress

Jasmine—very good for depression; uplifting and soothing

For Depression

Lemon—uplifting

Bergamot—relaxes the nervous system; good for anxiety; uplifting

For Motivation and Energy

Ginger—quickens and sharpens the senses; may help memory

Rosemary—clears the brain; may enhance memory

Peppermint—energizes

ESSENTIAL OILS

Essential oils are very strong and concentrated, so they should be mixed with a "carrier oil" such as almond oil (15 drops of the carrier oil to 4 ounces of essential oil). Just add a few drops of the essential oil and massage the body. You may also inhale using a steam inhaler or diffuser. Inhale the oil only for short periods of time.

People with medical conditions such as blood pressure problems or asthma may have reactions to essential oils, so consult your health care professional if you have any doubts.

Bath essential

Want an attitude change or a little more energy? Try a different aromatherapy bath each night of the week. You will be surprised at your fresher outlook on life. Some essences are stronger than others and are used for different effects. Simply count out a few drops of some common scents and get revitalized. Choose one or two of the following essential oils to put into your bath.[1]

- Restful bath—for maximum relaxation, use one of these essential oils: chamomile (2 drops), cypress (5 drops), orange blossom (2 drops), or lavender (6 drops)

- No-more-blahs bath—try lemon (4 drops), peppermint (4 drops), basil (3 drops), or bergamot (3 drops)

- Spicy bath—feel fresh with geranium (3 drops), lavender (6 drops), juniper (5 drops), or cardamom (4 drops)

- Wake-up bath—for a stimulating bath, use basil (3 drops), peppermint (4 drops), juniper (5 drops), hyssop (3 drops), or rosemary (5 drops)

- Tension bath—ease your way through the end of the week with bergamot (3 drops), geranium (3 drops), or lavender (6 drops)

Chapter 25

TIRED OR TOXIC?

Many fifty-year-olds who experience tiredness may not be truly fatigued. They may instead be toxic. The headaches, aches and pains, sinus problems, weight problems, foggy-headed feeling, intestinal gas, irregularity, and indigestion may be warning signs that indicate a need for detoxification. More and more evidence points to the accumulation of toxins as the cause of accelerated aging and chronic diseases at midlife.

We are the generation that has been exposed to more pollution than any other in history. By the time we reach fifty, we have consumed pounds of sugar, gallons of caffeinated beverages, and tons of processed and fast foods. Add in medications and the fact that we have not eaten with any sort of balance due to hectic lifestyles, coupled with a lack of fresh fruits and vegetables and not enough fiber to help move these toxins out of our systems, and you have the makings of autointoxification: self-poisoning. This occurs when the toxic buildup is so great that it recycles and enters the bloodstream, causing a myriad of uncomfortable symptoms that can baffle even the very best physician.

Clearing toxins from the body is a self-care procedure that is an important part of midlife preventative health care. Why is it that we are so toxic at this time of our lives? Considering all the steroids, antibiotics, pesticides, hormones, dyes, and waxes used in and on our food supply, it is no wonder these materials set off reactions in the body, causing a variety of health problems.

Toxicity can cause frequent illness, make us look older than our midlife years, and rob us of our vitality. As a matter of fact, many doctors and researchers now agree that degenerative conditions of the heart, colon, joints, and kidneys—as well as dizziness, depression, arthritis, insomnia, and immune suppression—may be the result of toxic accumulation in the body.

At fifty, our eliminative ability slows down as a result of this toxicity coupled with wastes of our own manufacture. Our bodies then become a virtual storehouse of pollutants. This leads to poor nutrient absorption because our polluted intestines cannot properly screen out chemicals or adequately filter food particles. This allows toxins to enter the bloodstream.

This scenario may even play a part in "leaky gut," or irritable bowel syndrome. If you are not eliminating properly (meaning you have less than two bowel movements per day, each and every day), you are constipated. Leaky gut gives the toxic wastes a chance to enter the bloodstream and create chronic unwellness or low energy. You have twenty-seven feet of intestinal tract. If you eat three times a day, plus snacks, just think of what occurs if you do not eliminate properly. Think of the amount of toxicity that builds as the food stagnates, ferments, and becomes putrefied. This may not a pleasant picture, but it is an illustration that you need in order to drive home the importance of cleansing your internal system.

One way to correct this problem is to cleanse your system twice a year, in the spring and the fall. A very easy, user-friendly way to do this would be to use an herbal formula that contains time-tested synergistic herbs that are system-specific, meaning herbs that cleanse the liver, blood, colon, and so on. When you take ancient herbal wisdom and marry it with the formulating technology of today, you have the benefit of a very efficient way to correct toxic overload and regain your health.

When it comes to detoxification, there are other ways to go besides herbal formulations: colonics, fasting, saunas, enemas, and juicing, for instance. But for ease, convenience, and effectiveness, herbal cleansing is found to be the most effective, provided you use a superior product.

Whichever product you use, remember that formulation is key. It must not be too harsh, and it must not consist of laxative herbs only. Find a formulation that contains system-specific herbs as well as herbs that help sweep the colon for the removal of toxins from your system. The process usually takes thirty to ninety days to gently eliminate years of accumulated waste matter. To further enhance the process, make sure that you clean up your diet and drink plenty of good-quality water.

After detoxification, many people feel as if they have been given their health back. Their skin clears up, elimination is regular, eyes sparkle, energy soars, vitality returns, digestion improves, aches and pains diminish or disappear, headaches become a thing of the past, and unhealthy cravings disappear.

Detoxification gives you a solid foundation upon which to build your health at fifty to a higher, more vibrant level! Again, at fifty you must take a measure of responsibility and do your part to help prevent some of the most debilitating diseases of our time. Become proactive. Detoxify your body, and add more life to your years!

Chapter 26

QUENCHING THE FIRE WITHIN

How do you manage chronic inflammation? The first step is to know your CRP levels. One of the most commonly used indicators of chronic inflammation is C-reactive protein (CRP), an acute-phase hepatic protein that rises rapidly in response to inflammation. It is commonly used to predict risk for cardiovascular disease but can also be used as a more general indicator of inflammation and disease risk. Elevated CRP levels have been shown to predict development of type 2 diabetes and are associated with numerous other health conditions.

Several factors contribute to chronic inflammation. They are as follows:

- Diet—evidence suggests that diets high in refined carbo-hydrates may contribute to chronic inflammation.

- Obesity—studies have shown that excess adipose tissue is associated with higher levels of CRP, while weight-loss studies demonstrate reductions in inflammatory markers.

- Sedentary lifestyle—can indirectly influence inflamma-tion through its promotion of weight gain and obesity.

- Smoking—smokers have higher CRP than nonsmokers.

How do you quench this fire within? Here are some suggestions:

- Weight loss—has been shown to reduce CRP levels.

- Physical activity—research suggests that physical activity can reduce inflammation.

- Mediterranean diet—one of the most effective dietary strategies for reducing inflammation with a generous intake of fruits, vegetables, whole grains, beans, nuts and seeds, olive oil, and deep-sea fish.

- Fatty acids—omega-3 fatty acids reduce the overall inflammatory burden.

- Curcumin—one of the most diverse and powerful natural anti-inflammatory agents known.

- Quercetin—used regularly in acute and chronic inflammatory conditions.

- Enzymes—proteases, papain, and bromelain.

- Boswellia—used in Ayurvedic medicine as an anti-inflammatory.

- Ginger—a spicy herb that has therapeutic properties for digestion, hypertension, headaches, and more. When it comes to inflammation, ginger is an effective inhibitor of the 5-LO enzyme, a chemical cousin of COX-2.

Chapter 27

MAGNESIUM MATTERS

In previous chapters I have written about GABA, L-theanine, and other nutrients that restore the brain. While GABA is the main inhibitory neurotransmitter that replenishes the brain, other nutrients also work along with GABA for its proper metabolism. One nutrient in particular is magnesium.

Magnesium enhances GABA's action and effect on the body. Interestingly enough, most people with long-standing anxiety and stress problems are deficient in magnesium. Furthermore, it is important to note that the symptoms of magnesium deficiency are the same as those that occur with anxiety, stress, and emotional depletion.

I have listed for you the symptoms of magnesium deficiency. (Note that there are many possible causes for these symptoms; if you have one or more of them, it does not necessarily signal magnesium deficiency.) They are:

- Depression

- Muscle spasms

- Anxiety

- Panic attacks

- Mitral valve prolapse

- Fibromyalgia

- Fatigue

- Low blood sugar

- Irregular heartbeat

- Dizziness

- Headaches

- Constipation

- Irritable bowel syndrome

- Asthma

- Spastic symptoms

- Chronic pain

- Noise sensitivity

MAGNESIUM MATTERS AT MIDLIFE

When you are rising to meet the demands and changes of being fifty, you are bound to encounter stress. When you are chronically stressed, you can become deficient in magnesium, even if you consume magnesium-rich foods on a daily basis.

When you are exposed to continuous stress—perhaps from taking care of an elderly parent or dealing with hormonal issues, teenagers, financial problems, marital problems, or anything else that this phase of life brings your way—you become irritable and easily fatigued, and you lose your ability to concentrate. Your blood pressure may begin to creep up because adrenaline levels increase in your blood.

It is under these conditions that magnesium is released from your blood cells and goes into your blood plasma. From there it is excreted in the urine. A study in France found that this stress-induced depletion of magnesium was more dramatic in those with type-A personalities, who were competitive and more prone to heart disease.[1] Some researchers suggest that this depletion of magnesium among type-A individuals may be the primary reason they carry an increased risk of heart attacks. It is also interesting to note that when an individual suffers a heart attack, magnesium is administered immediately.

In March 2003, the *American Journal of Cardiology* published some of the most convincing evidence that magnesium is truly relevant to heart health. One hundred eighty-seven people with CAD (coronary artery disease) who were given 365 mg of magnesium twice daily for a period of six months reported a "significant improvement" in their general pain levels. The placebo group saw no change at all.[2]

It has also been found that magnesium helps to regulate heart rhythms and thins the blood. Another benefit that magnesium provides is its ability to relax arteries, thereby lowering blood pressure.

A lack of magnesium can make matters worse when it comes to fifty-year-olds suffering from any of the following: type 2 diabetes, migraines, osteoporosis, anxiety, fibromyalgia, irregular heartbeat, irritable bowel syndrome, muscle spasms, low blood sugar, asthma, dizziness, panic attacks, chronic pain, constipation, mitral valve prolapse, and fatigue.

As Americans, we consume diets that fail to meet even the government's minimum recommended dietary allowance for magnesium. Again, most troubling is the inadequate intake among individuals who develop heart disease. In addition to adding the following foods to your midlife diet, I recommend that you supplement with 400 mg of magnesium at bedtime. It is the most critical of all minerals to take when coping with stress. Magnesium citrate is one of the most user-friendly forms.

Magnesium-rich foods include:

- Almonds
- Bananas
- Blackberries
- Black-eyed peas
- Broccoli
- Dates
- Green beans
- Kasha
- Kidney beans
- Millet
- Navy beans
- Shrimp
- Soybeans
- Tuna
- Watermelon

Note: People with kidney disease should consult their physician before taking more than the recommended daily allowance of magnesium (320 mg).

Chapter 28

THE ACID TEST

At fifty, we experience a decline in our natural ability to balance our acid-to-alkaline ratio. This can result in fatigue and low stamina. In our younger days, our bodies were busy keeping our systems slightly alkaline with buffering alkaline substances like minerals, bicarbonate, and oxygen. As we reach midlife, our body's ability to buffer weakens, which causes our tissues to become more acidic. This results in tiredness.

Lifestyle is another factor that makes our systems acidic. A lifestyle high in stress and low in relaxation creates more acidic wastes in your system. The standard American diet is very acidic. Refined sugar, chocolate, soft drinks, coffee, dairy, red meat, vinegar, and citrus all contain phosphorus and sulfur, both of which are acidic.

Food must be digested *before* it can become fuel for the body. At midlife, digestive enzyme supplementation is very important. (See chapter 10, "Digestive Health.") If you do not supplement with enzymes, your body will have to use a great deal of energy to break down your food, leaving you tired and even more acidic. Acidic bodies ache, are stiff, and are hard to live in. They may also be more prone to bladder infections, colds, flu, chronic illness, headaches, and digestive complaints. The following are tips to regain and maintain proper pH balance:

- Consume alkalinizing foods like tuna, salmon, melon, papaya, nuts, and seeds.

- Have a green drink daily to keep your system alkalinized; cleanse the bloodstream; detoxify the system; and supply the body with enzymes, minerals, and important nutrients.

- Eliminate coffee and alcohol.

You should also supplement with *sodium bicarbonate.* Sodium bicarbonate helps balance and normalize your acid/alkaline pH. This will boost your energy level and physical performance and will eliminate muscle fatigue. Dosage: dissolve ¼ teaspoon sodium bicarbonate in a glass of spring water every morning for one week; drink on an empty stomach. Discontinue if stomach pain occurs. *Do not* consume if your stomach is overly full from food or drink!

There is a slight possibility that you may become overly alkaline from taking sodium bicarbonate (tingling sensations, muscle spasms, and feeling overenergized). If so, simply stop taking the sodium bicarbonate and take 1 teaspoon of apple cider vinegar in water. Wait a couple of days before resuming the sodium bicarbonate.

ACID/ALKALINE SELF-TEST

The following self-test will help you to determine if you have tendencies toward acidity or alkalinity:[1]

- If you feel energized after eating meat, if you have strong bones and muscles, if you are a high-energy person, and if you have a healthy digestion, you may be *high alkaline.*

- If you have weak digestion, if you have muscle aches and pains, if you feel fatigued after a meat meal, and if you have weak bones and muscles, you may be *high acid.*

MIDLIFE ALKALINIZING BATH

This bath will alkalinize an overly acidic body. Remember, if you are suffering from too little sleep, high stress levels, poor diet, poor digestion, or poor elimination, or if you consume too much caffeine or alcohol or have frequent colds or flu, you are most likely too acidic. This bath will help you to feel energized and refreshed. It should be taken periodically to help keep your acid/alkaline level in balance.

Pain and stress can contribute to acidity in the body, which can set the stage for degenerative disease. Try this bath for some relief.

Alkalinizing Salt and Soda Bath

1 cup baking soda

2 cups sea salt

Add baking soda and sea salt to a tub of warm water. Get in and soak for twenty minutes (no more than twenty minutes or it may leave you exhausted). After the bath, wrap yourself in a cotton sheet and lie down for at least half an hour. Sip room-temperature water.

Chapter 29

DIABETES? HERE'S SWEET SUCCESS

Type 2 diabetes is often referred to as adult-onset diabetes because it often happens after age forty. It is the most common form of diabetes, affecting approximately 15 million people in this country alone.

Type 2 diabetes is characterized by the following symptoms: tiredness, weakness, weight loss, extreme thirst, extreme hunger, frequent urination, frequent infection, blurred vision, numbness, and pain in the extremities. The diagnosis can be made with a simple blood test that measures blood sugar levels. This test, referred to as a fasting blood sugar test (FBS), is performed in the morning before breakfast after a night of fasting. A test reading of more than 140 mg/dl is indicative of diabetes.

It is imperative to manage type 2 diabetes properly because long-term complications can occur, such as kidney failure, stroke, blindness, cardiovascular disease, neuropathy, and impotence.

At fifty, when so many other areas seem to need our attention and management, a newly diagnosed diabetic can feel overwhelmed at the prospect of managing yet another life-altering situation. Each type 2 diabetes patient's fate rests heavily on self-diagnosis, self-medication, dietary changes, emotional state, exercise, stress level, choices of therapeutic supplements, and more.

This disease demands a partnership between patient and doctor. Together they must work to first control and then manage and monitor blood sugar. If diabetes is managed well, complications can be avoided.

The diet for diabetics should be low in fat and high in fiber, with an emphasis on complex carbohydrates. If high blood pressure exists, reduce salt intake. Meals should be small to reduce the demand on one's system. Avoid alcohol and tobacco usage. High-protein diets should also be avoided to spare kidney function. Steps must be taken to minimize stress because stress raises blood sugar levels. Exercise is a great controller of diabetes and has even been known (when coupled with proper diet and weight loss) to actually return type 2 diabetics to normal blood sugar levels. Supplementation with high-potency, well-assimilated vitamins, minerals, herbs, and amino acids can contribute to the health and well-being of the diabetic patient.

YOUR PROTOCOL FOR DIABETES PREVENTION AND CONTROL

⭐ *Starred supplement: Alpha-lipoic acid*

Alpha-lipoic acid is an antioxidant that is important for the maintenance of neural health.[1]

> **Alpha-Lipoic Acid**
> Form: Capsule
> Dosage: 250 mg, taken with 2,500 mcg of biotin
> Frequency: Twice daily (for a total of 500 mg/day)

⭐ *Starred supplement: Chromium*

Chromium is an amino acid that increases the effects of insulin.[2]

Note: This protocol may decrease your need for insulin. Be sure to monitor your blood sugar levels carefully, as you may be able to decrease your dose of insulin. Work closely with your health care provider.

Chromium

Form: Capsule

Dosage: 200 mcg if you weigh less than 150 pounds; 400 mcg if you weigh 150 pounds or more

Frequency: Once daily

Second tier

It has been theorized that the following supplements may have beneficial effects for this condition of midlife:

- Vitamin E—antioxidant that widens blood vessels

- Vitamin C—immune-booster antioxidant

- Coenzyme Q_{10}—immune-booster antioxidant

- Grapeseed extract—most concentrated natural antioxidant

- Acetyl-L-carnitine—extremely important amino acid in the treatment of neuropathy

- Aspirin—amino acid that may prevent stroke by thinning the blood

- Biotin—mineral that enhances glucose utilization and neuropathy management[3]

- Magnesium—deficiency in this mineral occurs in up to 40 percent of diabetes patients; neuropathy and vascular damage can occur as a result of low magnesium

- Ginkgo biloba—antioxidant herb

- Ginger (not to be confused with wild ginger, which can be hazardous)—herb that inhibits abnormal platelet aggregation and reduces cholesterol

- Stevia extract—herbal sweetener that is safe for diabetic use; stevia is 60–100 times sweeter than sugar

- GLA (gamma-linolenic acid)—oil that regenerates capillaries and nourishes nerves

- EPA (eicosapentaenoic acid)—oil that reduces abnormal blood clotting and reduces triglyceride levels

For more information, contact the American Diabetes Association at 1-800-342-2383 or www.diabetes.org.

Chapter 30

MIDLIFE IMMUNITY

It is becoming increasingly difficult to keep our immune systems strong. This is especially true at fifty. Our immune systems deal with many pathogens on a daily basis (yeasts, parasites, fungi, and viruses) and many antigens (pollen, chemicals, drugs, malignant cells, and more). Without a strong immune system, we are more susceptible to illness.

The immune system is the greatest pharmacy in the world, making more than one hundred billion types of medicines (known as antibodies) to attack just about any unwanted germ or virus that enters your body. Best of all, none of the medicines made by your internal pharmacy produce side effects or cost anything, and they are the most powerful healing agents known to man.

Your immune system has only one requirement: the right raw materials to produce the internal medicines that safeguard you from illness. The following recommendations will help you to fortify yourself in times of stress and lighten the load on your immune system. They will detail what nutrients will support and strengthen immunity.

YOUR PROTOCOL FOR BOOSTING THE IMMUNE SYSTEM

⭐ *Starred supplement: Olive leaf extract*

Olive leaf extract is a powerful antiviral antimicrobial. Olive leaf contains oleuropein, which has been shown to be the source of its extremely potent disease-resistance properties.[1]

Olive Leaf Extract

Form: Capsule

Dosage: 250–500 mg

Frequency: As needed to boost immune system during bacterial, fungal, or viral illness

---

⭐ *Starred supplement: Coenzyme Q$_{10}$*

At least one study has shown that CoQ$_{10}$ has positive effects on the immune system.[2] CoQ$_{10}$ strengthens the body's immune response. It enhances the ability of immune cells to disable invading pathogens. Scientists believe it may even benefit people with various challenges to the immune system ranging from allergies to HIV infection.[3]

Coenzyme Q$_{10}$ (CoQ$_{10}$)

Form: Gelcap

Dosage: 100 mg

Frequency: Once daily

Second tier

It has been theorized the following supplements or procedures may have beneficial immune system boosting effects:

Natural supplements

- Green drink—have a cup of green tea or other green drink (such as Kyo-Green) daily.

- Moducare—plant sterol formula by Natural Balance

- Bio-K—liquid acidophilus

- Power mushrooms—maitake, shiitake, and/or reishi

- Astragalus

- B complex

- Milk thistle extract

- Plant enzymes—with each meal

- Ester-C—3,000 mg daily

- Garlic (Kyolic)[4]

Body work

- Rest enough.

- Stop smoking.

- Get massage therapy.

- Start to exercise.

- Get fifteen minutes of early morning sunlight daily.

- Laugh with friends.

- Practice deep breathing.

- Deepen your prayer life.

Dietary therapy

- Eat as close to the "original garden" as possible—plenty of fresh fruits and vegetables, high-fiber foods, seafood, yogurt, and kefir; add garlic and onions to your recipes for added immune-boosting benefit.

- Avoid sugary foods (pies, cakes), since these depress immunity.

- Avoid fried foods, red meat, and refined foods.

For more information on helping your immune system, I recommend that you read my book *90-Day Immune System Makeover.*

SUMMARY: YOUR IMMUNITY—WHAT CAN GO WRONG?

- Poor diet—consumption of refined sugar can interfere with immunity. According to the *American Journal of Clinical Nutrition,* a study found that sugar slowed the ability of the immune system to eradicate, engulf, and consume alien material.[5] Sugar's effect on insulin levels restricts vitamin C's role in allowing immune cells to travel and destroy invaders in our bodies.

- Lack of sleep—regeneration takes place while you sleep. Certain processes that rebuild during sleep do not take place during waking hours. Sleep experts tell us that while seven hours of sleep per night is the minimum amount needed for a properly functioning immune system, eight hours is still optimal.

- Alcohol—lowers immunity by inhibiting the ability of your white cells to react to infections.

- Stress—a study done in 1977 showed that blood taken from widows and widowers who were in the grieving process had reduced natural killer cell activity.[6] Stress and a depressed mental outlook can lower immunity.

- Being overweight—according to one study, a low-fat diet may help boost the activity of your natural killer cells, thereby enhancing your immune response.[7]

Chapter 31

YOUR BODY ON OVERDRIVE—
AUTOIMMUNE DISEASE

At fifty, many people are diagnosed with autoimmune diseases. There are several autoimmune conditions that can plague us at midlife. The most common are lupus, rheumatoid arthritis, allergies, and insulin-dependent diabetes. These can rob you of energy and stamina, cause pain, and limit your range of motion. They can damage major organs and tissues and wear you down emotionally, causing depression. Poor lifestyles especially can play a major role in the development of autoimmune diseases by the fifth decade of life. Lack of sleep, adrenal exhaustion, tobacco use, stress, caffeine, drugs, sugars, and poor diet can contribute to immune suppression. Oxidative damage from free radicals has also been implicated in the autoimmune disease process.

An autoimmune disease is characterized by the body's immune response being directed against its own tissues, which results in inflammation and destruction. In the case of rheumatoid arthritis, the body's own immune system mistakenly attacks the linings of joints. In insulin-dependent diabetes, the insulin-producing islet cells of the pancreas are attacked.

In a healthy body with a robust immune system, bacteria, viruses, and cancer cells are recognized by the body as abnormal and are attacked and destroyed. An immune system that is underactive, weakened, or defective can create havoc throughout the entire body, causing dangerous diseases.

One of the major contributors to immune dysfunction is stress. Even low levels of stress can encourage the adrenal glands to produce cortisol, which in turn impairs immune system function.

On a positive note, autoimmune diseases may be prevented by eating a healthy diet and boosting the autoimmune system with supplementation of specific nutrients. Those persons with existing autoimmune diseases can use supplementation to help suppress the inflammatory response.

Lifestyle and nutritional support for autoimmune diseases consists of getting regular exercise; sleeping enough; limiting stress; addressing thyroid health; decreasing oxidative damage by taking antioxidants such as vitamins A, C, E, and beta carotene; supplementing with essential fatty acids to decrease inflammation; and taking probiotics to support intestinal health. This must be done on a long-term basis for prevention or suppression of autoimmune system diseases.

Age is an important factor in the development of autoimmune system diseases. Education will arm you on how to prevent and combat it.

Chapter 32

WHERE DID THESE HEADACHES COME FROM?

At age fifty, headaches can be a common occurrence. Just look at all the television, magazine, and radio ads touting the benefits of using their analgesics. Stress and tension are at the top of the list when it comes to the etiology (causes) of the midlife headache. Drug companies have even created a "special blend" formula that addresses the headache brought on by tension. For women's midlife headaches, there is a good chance that stress, tension, and hormonal imbalance from perimenopause or menopause are triggering the head thumpers.

There are many ways to limit or eliminate the occurrence of the midlife headache. Dietary recommendations are to remove chocolate, caffeine, dairy, wheat, nuts, and soy from your diet for two weeks to determine if a food sensitivity is causing your headaches. Taking 300–400 mg of magnesium at bedtime may help prevent tight, tense muscles.

In women, estrogen dominance is usually the culprit. Consider using natural progesterone cream to balance the ratio of estrogen to progesterone. Many women find blessed relief once the ratio is back in balance. The cream may be applied directly to the temples or the back of the neck at the onset of or during a headache.

Chapter 33

SMILE! YOU'RE FIFTY—
PERIODONTAL HEALTH

Periodontal disease begins with a gradual process involving plaque buildup under the gum line. This causes swollen and bleeding gums, also known as gingivitis. This process can lead to chronic inflammation and infection by allowing bacteria to pass into the bloodstream, where systemic disease can develop.

Many fifty-year-olds visit their dentists as their smiles begin to look dingy and yellow. They are hoping for teeth-whitening procedures and/or cosmetic dentistry. But the fact is that a pretty smile should not be the only motivation for keeping gums healthy. It is a vital part of proactive antiaging health maintenance.

YOUR PROTOCOL FOR PERIODONTAL HEALTH

⭐ *Starred supplement: Coenzyme Q$_{10}$*

According to one study, our old friend CoQ_{10} has been shown to protect against periodontal disease.[1] Periodontal pocket depth decreased and gum healing improved after six weeks of topical use. CoQ_{10} is considered the number one therapy to treat periodontal disease from the inside out.

Coenzyme Q_{10} (CoQ_{10})

Form: Gelcap

Dosage: 100 mg

Frequency: Once daily

Second tier

It has been theorized that the following supplements may have beneficial effects for this condition:

- Propolis extract—natural antibiotic to reduce gum inflammation[2]

- Vitamin E—prevents free-radical damage to gums and mucous membranes caused by infection and abrasion

- Green tea—neutralizes free radicals in the mouth and protects against infections and dental cavities[3]

- Folic acid—specific antigingivitis therapy when applied topically, according to five published studies[4]

- Stevia—new noncaloric herbal sweetener

- Pau d'arco—an anti-infective

- Peppermint oil—cleanses and refreshes

Prevention

- Brush teeth thoroughly after meals or at least twice daily.

- Floss daily.

- Visit your dentist two to four times yearly.

Chapter 34

HEALTHY BRAIN, HEALTHY MIND

At fifty, it is important to replenish and rejuvenate the brain. If you experience memory lapses, moodiness, depression, spaciness, poor concentration, anxiety, and forgetfulness, you are not alone. In this day and age, stress is taking a toll on our brain health and balance. We Americans are overworked, burned out, and stressed out, and we never get enough much-needed, rejuvenating downtime. Stress depletes the brain and body of amino acids (the building blocks of protein) and potassium, contributing to mental burnout.

You must feed your brain to replenish and restore optimal brain function. Brain nutrients can quickly improve brain performance, correcting many emotional and physical symptoms, as well.

YOUR PROTOCOL FOR BRAIN HEALTH

⭐ *Starred supplement: Phosphatidylserine*

After the age of forty-five, phosphatidylserine supplementation can help enhance memory and mental alertness. This brain nutrient helps maintain healthy cognitive function, thereby clearing up brain fog and mental confusion, helping restore lost trains of thought, and preventing the tendency toward misplaced car keys. In addition, phosphatidylserine supports cognitive function, emotional well-being, and behavioral performance by restoring cell membrane composition.[1]

Phosphatidylserine

Form: Capsule

Dosage: 300 mg (in divided doses)

Frequency: 300 mg daily (in divided doses)

⭐ Starred supplement: GABA

Of all the inhibitory neurotransmitters in the brain, GABA (gamma-aminobutyric acid) is the most widely distributed. It has a very important part to play in the regulation of anxiety, according to Michael J. Gitlin, MD, and in the restoration of brain health.

I used GABA to replenish my brain and thereby calm my mind and body. Its effect was truly amazing. With my GABA receptors replenished, the false alarms and overfiring stopped, and the panic attacks I had endured for over five years ceased. I began to recommend it to my clients who had continued to have mind and body symptoms long after they completed their nutritional programs. The results were no less than remarkable.

GABA proved to be a valuable piece of the puzzle in regulating my emotional balance and freedom from anxiety and stress-related illness. This was because the GABA receptors in the area of the brain that control anxiety became replenished and restored after supplementation with this simple amino acid. Why not take this simple amino acid to replenish your brain? It has no risks or side effects.

GABA stores must be replaced on a regular basis since anxiety, pain, and grief are daily occurrences and deplete the GABA reserves. GABA should be replenished each day. It improves brain function and reduces anxiety. If it is taken with meals or near mealtimes, it will be digested along with other amino acids and be used by the body as a building block to repair or make new skin cells. For best results for brain health, though, GABA should be taken on an empty stomach or at bedtime.

Research conducted at the Pain and Stress Center in San Antonio with patients suffering from all types of stress, pain, muscle spasms, or anxiety/panic attacks demonstrated that pure GABA (375 or 750 mg) can mimic the tranquilizing effects of Valium or Librium without the possibility of addiction or fear of being sedated.[2]

Note: Always take GABA with at least 10 mg of vitamin B_6. Also, taking 200 mg of magnesium can enhance the results of GABA.

GABA

Form: Capsule (may be opened and dissolved in water; relief should come in 10–12 minutes)

Dosage: 375 or 750 mg

Frequency: Up to three times daily, as needed

Second tier

It has been theorized the following supplements may have beneficial brain health boosting effects:

- Omega-3 oils

- DHA oils

- EPA oils

- Lecithin

- Brewer's yeast

- Royal jelly

- Ginkgo biloba

- 5-HTP—at bedtime to boost serotonin

- Glutamine

- Glycine

- Magnesium—800 mg gelcaps or 10–15 drops of liquid magnesium chloride

- Flax oil

- Coenzyme Q_{10}—with vitamin E, 60–100 mg daily

- B complex

- L-theanine

Also, add the following foods to your diet:

- Eggs

- Olive oil

- Brown rice

- Wheat germ

- Apples

- Leafy greens

Healthy lifestyle habits

- Exercise.

- Practice deep breathing.

- Listen to soothing music.

- Avoid alcohol.

- Avoid tobacco.

- Avoid sugar.

You can also do crossword puzzles to build more brain circuits.

AMINO ACIDS FOR BRAIN AND BODY FUNCTION

Amino acids and brain function go hand in hand. Understanding your brain function will give you a more comprehensive picture of how various amino acids are effective for the treatment of pain, stress, anxiety, and depression. Your body needs and uses basic nutrients every day. These include vitamins, minerals, proteins, carbohydrates, and fats. If you were to take the water and fat out of your body, 75 percent of what would remain would be protein. Muscles, cell membranes, enzymes, and neurotransmitters are all proteins.

Amino acids make up proteins found in every tissue of the body and play a major role in nearly every chemical process affecting physical and mental function. As a result, amino acids have more diverse functions than other nutrients. They contribute to the formation of proteins, muscles, neurotransmitters, enzymes, antibodies, and receptors. Amino acids are involved in basic cellular energy production. Amino acid imbalances can manifest as a variety of symptoms and metabolic disorders at midlife.

Below are some symptoms of amino acid deficiencies.[3] (Note that if you have one or more of these symptoms, it does not necessarily mean you have amino acid deficiencies.)

SYMPTOMS OF AMINO ACID DEFICIENCIES

Behavioral disorders	Mood swings
Candida infections	Panic attacks
Aggression	Chronic fatigue (emotional/physical)
Immune system disorders	Cardiovascular disease
Vitamin and mineral deficiencies	Seizures
Eating disorders	Osteoarthritis
Hypoglycemia	Muscle weakness
Diabetes	Poor concentration
Phobias	Food and chemical sensitivity
Rheumatoid arthritis	Neurological disorders
Digestive disorders	Anxiety
Chronic pain	ADD/hyperactivity
Chronic allergies	Cancer
Mental confusion	Fear
Digestive disorders	Headaches
Learning disorders	IBS (irritable bowel syndrome)
Depression	Substance abuse

You can determine any specific amino acid deficiencies you may have by having a twenty-panel amino acid blood test (fasting plasma) drawn. Consult an orthomolecular health care professional.

REPLENISHING THE BRAIN THROUGH AMINO ACIDS

L-theanine is an amino acid found in green tea that produces tranquilizing effects in the brain. For centuries, green tea has been used in the Orient for its calming, curative properties without drowsiness. L-theanine increases GABA, which increases well-being. Look for Suntheanine from Taiyo International, Inc., the only pure form available.[4]

Note: While GABA and L-theanine may be taken together, you may want to start with L-theanine to see if you need to add GABA.

Lysine is an essential amino acid that is effective in the natural treatment of hypothyroidism, Alzheimer's disease, and Parkinson's disease.

Glutamine is an amino acid that is a prime brain nutrient and energy source. Supplementing your brain with glutamine may rapidly improve memory, recall, concentration, and alertness. It helps to reduce sugar and alcohol cravings and controls hypoglycemic reactions.

Tyrosine is a wonderful semi-essential amino acid formed from phenylalanine. Tyrosine helps to build the body's natural supply of adrenaline and thyroid hormones. It is also an antioxidant and is a source of quick energy, especially for the brain. Because it converts in the body to the amino acid L-dopa, it is considered a safe, natural support for Parkinson's disease, depression, and hypertension. If you have cancerous melanoma or manic depression, you should avoid tyrosine.

Glycine helps to release growth hormone when taken in large doses. It converts to creatine in the body to retard nerve and muscle degeneration. It is wonderful for controlling and regulating hypoglycemic sugar drops, and it is especially effective when taken in the morning upon rising.

Taurine is a potent antiseizure amino acid. This neurotransmitter helps control the nervous system and hyperactivity, normalizes irregular heartbeat, helps prevent circulatory and heart disorders, and helps lower cholesterol. Since natural sources of taurine are hard to find, supplementation is the best way to receive adequate amounts for therapeutic benefit.

GUIDELINES FOR TAKING AMINO ACIDS

- Take amino acids with their nutrient cofactors (such as vitamin B_6 and vitamin C) for the best uptake and absorption.

- Take individual amino acids in the morning, before meals, or between meals so they won't compete for absorption with amino acids in foods.

- Make sure to take amino acids with plenty of water for optimum absorption.

Please note that only active forms of amino acids are available for sale, so even if you do not see an "L-" (levo) or "D-" (dextro) before the amino acid name, the product is still the active form. *Example:* L-carnitine or carnitine.

OVERTAXING THE LEFT AND RIGHT SIDES OF YOUR BRAIN

While writing this book I came across an interesting article entitled "The Brain's Balancing Act."[5] In essence, the article said that working either the left or right side of your brain too hard can wreak havoc on your whole body. By stimulating the underused portion of your brain, you can restore balance. When your brain is in balance, your well-being increases and your health receives immediate benefit.

Let's examine this theory. The left side of the human brain sees individual parts that make up a whole. It organizes, analyzes, and rationalizes information. It is also the verbal side of your brain, responding to speech and using words to name and describe things. It keeps track of time and thinks in terms of consequences. In contrast, the right side of the brain addresses emotions and is affected by music, touch, and body language. It follows hunches and feelings rather than logic. It is the visual side of your brain. It responds to pictures, colors, and shapes.

Overreliance on one side of the brain or the other can create frustration and eventual brain burnout. What affects the brain also affects the body, so brain burnout can lead to physical problems, such as insomnia, headaches, and fatigue. A body cannot be healthy if the brain is not in balance.

Below I have included a chart based on information developed by Ann McCombs, DO, who works with brain hemisphericity. She has found that certain symptoms may indicate a brain imbalance. Most symptoms are left- or right-side specific. There are, however, some signs that could indicate a strain of either side.

BALANCING YOUR BRAIN
Signs That the Right Brain May Be Overtaxed
Staring off into space
Feelings of panic
Difficulty paying attention
Feeling overly sensitive and emotional
For Right Brain Relief
Work on a crossword puzzle
Organize your closet
Play a game of logic (like chess)
Learn new software
Develop a personal budget
Signs That the Left Brain May Be Overtaxed
Feelings of worry
Difficulty communicating
Inability to follow a schedule
Difficulty solving problems

BALANCING YOUR BRAIN
For Left Brain Relief
Dance
Listen to music
Cook or make a gourmet dish
Play with your children
Watch a movie
Take a walk outdoors

GROWING OLDER: INEVITABLE.
FEELING OLDER: OPTIONAL!

Fifty-year-olds belong to a mass movement of people who are refusing to go quietly into middle age. Instead of becoming victims of a collective midlife meltdown, I say we can take the yearnings and desires of our hearts, along with the dissatisfactions and deep questions, and turn them all into one big call to action!

Men and women age fifty and over are reinventing and redefining their lives, swapping careers, launching new businesses, bicycling around the world, and competing in triathlons. This generation has always believed in dreaming big. We are reshaping midlife for future generations and literally making fifty the new thirty. I am honored to be among the ranks of forerunners who at fifty are confident enough in their judgment and comfortable enough in their skin to master the art of traveling light, which will enable us to rediscover our creativity, ingenuity, and courage to make life *fabulous at fifty*!

Won't you join us?

FIFTY WAYS TO
EXTEND YOUR DAYS

T he following is a list of fifty lifestyle changes, vitamins, minerals, and herbs that will not only help to extend your days but add more vibrant life to your years, redefine your aging process, and make your fifty fabulous.

1. *Cancer prevention: Indole-3-carbinol*

Indole-3-carbinol is a powerful phytochemical found in cruciferous vegetables, providing breast, cervical, and prostate cell support by activating detoxification enzymes, promoting healthy estrogen balance and cellular metabolism, and scavenging free radicals.[1]

2. *Mood elevator: 5-HTP*

5-hydroxytryptophan is derived from the griffonia simplicifolia plant. Supplementation with 5-HTP encourages brain serotonin levels that can lead to positive effects on emotional well-being, appetite control, and sleep/wake cycles. Clinical studies have shown that 5-HTP increases serotonin levels.[2]

3. *Antianxiety: L-theanine*

L-theanine is an amino acid derived from green tea that has been recognized for centuries as having relaxant properties. In addition to promoting relaxation, L-theanine helps to moderate occasional stress and the effects of caffeine on the central nervous system. L-theanine is a unique amino acid that eases irritability and nervous tension without causing drowsiness.[3]

4.   Natural hormone replacement: Black cohosh

Black cohosh (*cimicifuga racemosa*) offers support during menopause and reduces hot flashes. It helps maintain healthy levels of LH (luteinizing hormone), which contributes to physical well-being. Black cohosh has mild estrogenic properties by binding to estrogen receptors, thereby supporting healthy estrogen levels during menopause.[4]

5.   Joint health midlife marvel: Glucosamine, chondroitin, MSM

This trio of substances—glucosamine, chondroitin, and MSM— helps to strengthen cartilage and promote comfortable joint movement. These naturally occurring substances build and maintain the matrix of collagen and connective tissue that forms the ground substance of cartilage.[5]

6.   Prostate support: Lycopene

Lycopene is a natural tomato extract. Studies show that lycopene from consumption of tomato or tomato-based products may help digestive, lung, stomach, cervical, prostate, and breast health. In a study involving thirty male subjects, supplementation with lycopene promoted healthy prostate function. It is interesting to note that the study also found that lycopene supplementation, rather than dietary tomato consumption, supported prostate health. In addition, lycopene is an antioxidant that supports cellular health.[6]

7.   Stress, cardiovascular, immune, cognitive, and joint health: Ashwaganda

Ashwaganda is a four-thousand-year-old adaptogenic herb that belongs to the pepper family. In animal studies, ashwaganda has been shown to support the activity of lymphocytes and macrophages, moderate occasional stress, enhance memory and cognitive function, provide neuroprotection by scavenging free radicals, and support thyroid function. Ashwaganda's adaptogenic properties provide multi-functional support for promoting mental and physical wellness, occasional stress, and healthy lipid and glucose metabolism.[7]

8. Nerve health and glucose metabolism: Alpha-lipoic acid

Alpha-lipoic acid is a potent antioxidant that neutralizes harmful free radicals and enhances the activity of vitamins C and E. It is a key player in the metabolic process that produces energy in muscles and directs calories into energy production. In addition, alpha-lipoic acid supports the nervous system and provides support for healthy liver function. It also helps to sustain normal blood sugar levels and promotes healthy glucose metabolism in both lean and overweight persons.[8]

9. Healthy lipid metabolism: Policosanol

Policosanol is derived from sugar cane. It supports cardiovascular health, provides antioxidant protection, promotes healthy platelet function, and supports healthy lipid metabolism. Policosanol is a well-tolerated supplement that has been the subject of both short- and long-term research over the past decade.[9]

10. Cardiovascular protection: CoQ$_{10}$

CoQ$_{10}$ provides benefits for cardiovascular health (recommended by many cardiologists), gum disease, prostate, and breast cancer protection. Additionally, CoQ$_{10}$ offers the following health benefits: immune health, skin health, cognitive and nerve health, cellular health, and cranial vascular health.

11. Antiaging super food: Royal jelly

Royal jelly is a super food for antiaging that stimulates immunity and deep cellular health, boosts circulation to the skin, and supplies key nutrients, like pantothenic acid, for energy and mental alertness.

12. Immune support: Zinc

Zinc helps to limit free radicals your body naturally produces and plays an important role in supporting the body's defense system. Zinc plays a fundamental role in collagen formation and healthy tissue development. This mineral also contributes to healthy prostatic function.

13. Powerful antioxidant: Oligomeric proanthocyanidins (OPC)

OPCs are powerful antioxidants that strengthen capillaries and connective tissue. They reduce LDL cholesterol that can accumulate in arteries, which can contribute to atherosclerosis.

14. Antioxidant for immune system support: Selenium

Selenium is both an antioxidant and a trace mineral that protects the body from heavy metal toxicity, increases glutathione, and reduces the risk of cancers, such as lung, esophagus, prostate, and colorectal cancers.

15. Primary antioxidant: Vitamin C

Vitamin C boosts immunity. It is a primary antioxidant that offers protection against heart disease, allergies, cancer, high blood pressure, arthritis, and infection. In addition, it safeguards against toxic heavy metals, radiation, and pollutants.

16. Arterial protection: Bioflavonoids

Bioflavonoids are a natural anti-inflammatory component of vitamin C that prevent hardening of the arteries; strengthen connective tissue, veins, and capillaries; and helps control bruising. In addition, bioflavonoids help stimulate bile for better digestion and help lower cholesterol.

17. Antiaging antioxidant: Vitamin E

Vitamin E is an antiaging antioxidant that reduces the risk of heart attack by acting as an anticoagulant and vasodilator against blood clots. It retards cellular and mental aging.

18. Potent antioxidant: Tocotrienols

Tocotrienols are compounds related to vitamin E's tocopherols that have powerful antioxidant effects, lower cholesterol, and have anti-cancer properties. In addition, tocotrienols protect against damage to the arterial walls and have a strong lipid-lowering ability.

19. Prime immune booster: L-glutathione

L-glutathione is an antioxidant amino acid that works to neutralize radiation and/or drug toxicity and inhibits free radical formation. A potent detoxifier, it cleanses the blood from the effects of liver toxins, chemotherapy, and X-rays. In addition, it is protective against age-related eye disease, such as macular degeneration and cataracts.

20. Antiaging brain and energy stimulant: Ginkgo biloba

The ginkgo leaf is shaped like the human brain. Interestingly enough, ginkgo biloba has been confirmed to boost circulation to the brain, improving memory and cognitive function. It is widely used in Europe and Asia as a longevity tonic.

21. Anti-inflammatory: Turmeric

Turmeric has a bold yellow-orange color that is familiar to anyone who has eaten curry. As in traditional Indian medicine, turmeric is used to treat arthritis, bursitis, and tendonitis. It also improves circulation!

22. Heart health: Hawthorn

European studies have confirmed hawthorn's cardiovascular benefits, which includes lowering blood pressure during exertion, strengthening the heart muscle, and improving blood flow to the heart and throughout the entire body. It has also been shown to aid in lowering cholesterol.

23. Antiaging brain nutrient: Acetyl-L-carnitine

Acetyl-L-carnitine is an amino acid that reduces age-related mental decline and increases alertness, attention span, and memory-learning ability.

24. Broad spectrum adaptogenic herb: Panax ginseng

Panax ginseng is an antiaging wonder that increases energy and stamina. It has been used medically in Asia for over five thousand years. It is considered an "adaptogen," meaning it enhances body functions and the immune system to help people adapt to the negative effects of stress, both mental and physical.

25. Breathe well

Proper breathing will help you relax. Start from the very bottom of your lungs and breathe in slowly through your nose.

26. Take "mini-vacations"

Take thirty-second mental vacations daily. Wander mentally through your favorite places in this beautiful world—a white sand beach, a park, the mountains—or remember the gaze of a loved one.

27. Sleep

Develop a regular sleep pattern. Reduce caffeine intake (especially late in the day), reduce alcohol, and avoid eating large, fatty meals that will keep you up at night. Try to aim for eight hours of sleep nightly.

28. Pray

Worry and anxiety stand between us and real rest and health. Turn your cares over to your Creator in prayer and trust that He will take care of you. He will not fail you, because He cannot!

29. Laugh

Laughter is truly the best medicine! Through laughter, blood pressure goes down, muscles relax, and the brain releases endorphins that make you feel great!

30. Stretch

Include stretching each day as a part of your balanced exercise program. Focus on everyday activities that will increase movement, such as taking the stairs instead of the elevator, mowing the grass, mopping and vacuuming floors, and playing with children.

31. Together time

The key to building strong, trusting relationships is spending time together.

32. Read uplifting books

33. Get to know the people you admire

Ask questions, listen, and follow their lead.

34. Work

Do not neglect valuable relationships with co-workers. Learn about their families and their dreams. This may in turn make your work environment less stressful and more enriching.

35. Prioritize

Look at out-of-balance areas in your life and choose your priorities.

36. Act

Once you have chosen your priorities, set your goals and take action!

37. Sight

Add beautiful sights to your personal world. Watch a sunset, plant flowers, or surround yourself with blooming plants.

38. Sound

Add beautiful music and peaceful sounds to your life. This will help you feel relaxed and at peace even when stressed.

39. Touch

Give and ask for hugs—lots of them. Have a massage and take hot baths at the end of long days.

40. Taste

Enjoy new flavors, cook with new spices, and eat all of the colors in nature!

41. Smell

Boost your health with aromatherapy—vanilla, lavender, cinnamon, and the like. Buy candles, flowers, and potpourri.

42. Find an exercise partner

It's more fun to exercise with someone, and it motivates you to continue your exercise program.

43. Aerobic exercise

Strengthen your heart and lungs with aerobic exercise. Don't forget to warm up and cool down.

44. Strength-train

To improve overall strength and endurance of muscles, be sure to include strength-training in your exercise routine.

45. Tell your family you love them—every day!

46. Do not make big decisions...

...when you are tired, lonely, angry, or hungry.

47. Don't go back for "seconds"

48. Drink six to eight glasses of pure water every day.

49. Commit to live the life God intended for you—one of health, happiness, and purpose!

50. Commit to continued improvement in all areas of your health and relationships!

Notes

INTRODUCTION TO PART • MAKING FIFTY THE NEW THIRTY!

1. Dr. Maoshing Ni, *Secrets of Longevity*, "The Yellow Emperor's Classic of Medicine" (San Francisco: Chronicle Books, 2006), 10.

CHAPTER 1 • REDEFINING THE AGING PROCESS

1. Dorrie Edelstein, "Support for Caregivers," Family Matters, *Ladies' Home Journal*, November 2003, 40.

2. Dr. Hap LeCrone, "Change Is Essential for a Healthy 2nd Half of Life," Senior Living, *Daytona Beach News Journal*, October 5, 2003.

CHAPTER 2 • ZAPPING THE BIG EIGHT AGE-MAKERS

1. *Life Extension*, "Delaying the Onset of Degenerative Diseases," supplemental edition, December 2003, 34–36.

2. Federico Parodi et al., "Oral Administration of Diferuloylmethane (Curcumin) Suppresses Proinflammatory Cytokines and Destructive Connective Tissue Remodeling in Experimental Abdominal Aortic Aneurysms," *Annals of Vascular Surgery* 20, no. 3 (May 2006): 360–368.

3. F. Suarez et al., "Pancreatic Supplements Reduce Symptomatic Response of Healthy Subjects to a High Fat Meal," *Digestive Disease Sciences* 44, no. 7 (July 1999): 1317–1321; Brad Rachman, "Unique Features and Application of Non-Animal Derived Enzymes," *Clinical Nutrition Insights* 5, no. 10 (1997), 1–4; K. Odea, "Factors Influencing Carbohydrate Digestion: Acute and Long Term Consequences," *Diabetes, Nutrition & Metabolism* 3 (1990): 251–258; J. Schick et al., "Two Distinct Adaptive Responses in the Synthesis of Exocrine Pancreatic Enzymes to Inverse Changes in Protein and Carbohydrate in the Diet," *American Journal of Physiology: Gastrointestinal and Liver Physiology* 247, no. 6 (December 1984): G611–G616.

4. V. E. Kagan et al., "Dihydrolipoic Acid—a Universal Antioxidant Both in the Membrane and in the Aqueous Phase. Reduction of Peroxyl, Ascorbyl and Chromanoxyl Radicals," *Biochemical Pharmacology* 44, no. 8 (October 1992): 1637–1649.

5. G. Tate et al., "Suppression of Acute and Chronic Inflammation by Dietary Gamma-Linolenic Acid," *Journal of Rheumatology* 16, no. 6 (June 1989): 729–734; T. H. Lee et al., "Effects of Dietary Fish Oil Lipids on Allergic and Inflammatory Diseases," *Allergy Proceedings* 12, no. 5 (September–October 1991): 299–303.

6. S. Lee-Huang et al., "Anti-HIV Activity of Olive Leaf Extract (OLE) and Modulation of Host Cell Gene Expression by HIV-1 Infection and OLE Treatment," *Biochemical and Biophysical Research Communications* 307, no. 4 (August 2003): 1029–1037; T. H. Abdullah et al., "Enhancement of Natural Killer Cell Activity in AIDS With Garlic," *Dtsch Zsohr Onkol* 21 (1989): 52–53.

7. L. A. Braam et al., "Vitamin K_1 Supplementation Retards Bone Loss in Postmenopausal Women Between 50 and 60 Years of Age," *Calcified Tissue International* 73, no. 1 (July 2003): 21–26; K. G. Jie et al., "Vitamin K Status and Bone Mass in Women With and Without Aortic Atherosclerosis: A Population-Based Study," *Calcified Tissue International* 59, no. 5 (November 1996): 352–356.

8. E. P. Quinlivan et al., "Importance of Both Folic Acid and Vitamin B_{12} in Reduction of Risk of Vascular Disease," *Lancet* 359 (January 2002): 227–228.

CHAPTER 3 • HEALTHY AGING: ADD MORE LIFE TO YOUR YEARS!

1. Bottom Line, *Super Healing Unlimited* (Stamford, CT: Bottom Line Books, 2006), 399.

2. T. Muller et al., "Coenzyme Q_{10} Supplementation Provides Mild Symptomatic Benefit in Patients With Parkinson's Disease," *Neuroscience Letters* 341 (2003): 201–204; S. Greenberg and W. H. Frishman, "Coenzyme Q_{10}: A New Drug for Cardiovascular Disease," *Journal of Clinical Pharmacology* 30, no. 7 (July 1990): 596–608.

3. K. P. High, "Nutritional Strategies to Boost Immunity and Prevent Infection in Elderly Individuals," *Clinical Infectious Diseases* 33, no. 11 (December 2001): 1892–1900, as quoted by Darin Ingels, ND, "Multivitamin Boosts Immune System in Middle-Aged Adults," *Health Notes Newswire*, March 28, 2002, http://www.emersonecologics .com/Newswire.asp?id=305 (accessed April 5, 2007).

4. Wei Zheng and Shiow Y. Wang, "Antioxidant Activity and Phenolic Compounds in Selected Herbs," *Journal of Agricultural and Food Chemistry* 49, no. 11 (2001): 5165–5170, as summarized in Rosalie Marion Bliss, "Herbs Can Spice Up Your Antioxidant Protection," Agricultural Research Service, February 12, 2002, http://www.ars .usda.gov/is/pr/2002/020212.htm (accessed March 22, 2007).

5. Jeff E. Poulin et al., "Vitamin E Prevents Oxidative Modification of Brain and Lymphocyte Band 3 Proteins During Aging," *Proceedings of the National Academy of Sciences* 93, no. 11 (May 1996): 5600–5603.

6. DicQie Fuller, *The Healing Power of Enzymes* (New York: Forbes Custom Publishing, 1998), 118.

7. Michael F. Roizen, MD, *Real Age Makeover* (New York: Harper Collins, 2005), 60–63.

CHAPTER 4 • BEATING STRESS BEFORE IT BEATS YOU

1. Bristol-Myers Squibb Company, *What Is Anxiety?* (Princeton, NJ: Bristol-Myers Squibb Co., 1996).

2. T. H. Holmes and R. H. Rahe, "The Social Readjustment Rating Scale," *Journal of Psychosomatic Research* 11 (1967): 214. Used by permission.

3. Sandra Blakeslee, "Complex and Hidden Brain in Gut Makes Stomachaches and Butterflies," *New York Times*, January 23, 1996, C1.

4. Mary A. Fristad, PhD, director of research and psychological services, Division of Child and Adolescent Psychiatry, Ohio State University Medical Center.

CHAPTER 5 • THE PAUSE THAT REFRESHES—SLEEP

1. E. U. Vorbach et al., "Therapy for Insomnia: Efficacy and Tolerability of a Valerian Preparation. 600 mg of Valerian," *Psychopharmakotherapie* 3 (1996): 109–115.

CHAPTER 8 • GETTING TO THE HEART OF THE MATTER— CARDIOVASCULAR HEALTH

1. G. P. Oakley, "Eat Right and Take a Multivitamin," *New England Journal of Medicine* 338 (April 1998): 1060–1061.

2. S. Greenberg and W. H. Frishman, "Coenzyme Q_{10}: A New Drug for Cardiovascular Disease," *Journal of Clinical Pharmacology* 30 (July 1990): 596–608.

3. J. M. Whitaker, MD, Citizen Petition Before the Department of Health and Human Services, Food and Drug Administration, November 24, 2002.

4. J. B. Ubbink, "Vitamin B-12, Vitamin B-6, and Folate Nutritional Status in Men With Hyperhomocysteinemia," *American Journal of Clinical Nutrition* 57 (January 1993): 47–53.

5. K. G. Losonczy, T. B. Harris, and R. J. Havlik, "Vitamin E and Vitamin C Supplement Use and Risk of All-Cause and Coronary Heart Disease Mortality in Older Persons: The Established Populations for Epidemiologic Studies of the Elderly," *American Journal of Clinical Nutrition* 64 (1996): 190–196.

6. O. Petrowicz et al., "Effects of Artichoke Leaf Extract (ALE) on Lipoprotein Metabolism in Vitro and in Vivo," *Atherosclerosis* 129 (1997): 147.

7. Joshua Backon, "Ginger: Inhibition of Thromboxane Synthetase and Stimulation of Prostacyclin: Relevance for Medicine and Psychiatry," *Medical Hypothesis* 20 (July 1986): 271–278.

8. *Indian Journal of Medical Research* 87 (1988): 356–360, as quoted in Health Marketplace, "Herbal Cardiovascular Formula,"

http://www.health-marketplace.com/Herbal-Cardiovascular-Formula
.htm (accessed March 22, 2007).

9. *Nutrition Research* 7 (1987): 139–149, as quoted in *Life Extension*, "Garlic," October 1998, http://www.lef.org/magazine/mag98/oct98_report1.html (accessed March 22, 2007).

10. R. Srivastava et al., "Effect of Curcumin on Platelet Aggregation and Vascular Prostacyclin Synthesis," *Arzniem-Forsh* 36 (1986): 715–717.

11. K. Srinivasan et al., "The Effects of Spices on Cholesterol 7 Alpha-Hydroxylase Activity and on Serum and Hepatic Cholesterol Levels in the Rat," *International Journal for Vitamin and Nutrition Research* 61, no. 4 (1991): 364–369.

12. *Journal of Lipid Mediators and Cell Signaling* (Netherlands) 17, no. 3 (1977): 207–220, as quoted in *Life Extension*, "The Unique Benefits of Perilla Oil," November 1998, http://www.lef.org/magazine/mag98/nov98_perilla2.html (accessed March 22, 2007).

CHAPTER 9 • DO I LOOK FAT?

1. Y. Park et al., "Effect of Conjugated Linoleic Acid on Body Composition in Mice," *Lipids* 32, no. 8 (August 1997): 853–858.

2. U. Risérus, L. Berglund, and B. Vessby, "Conjugated Linoleic Acid (CLA) Reduced Abdominal Adipose Tissue in Obese Middle-aged Men With Signs of the Metabolic Syndrome: A RandomisedControlled Trial," *International Journal of Obesity and Related Metabolic Disorders* 25, no. 8 (August 2001): 1129–1135.

3. Dr. David G. Williams, "New Health Breakthroughs From Around the World," *Alternatives* newsletter, vol. 8, no. 21 (Rockville, MD.: Mountain Home Publishing), 12–13.

4. Ellen J. Kamhi, PhD, with Dorrie Greenblatt, "Relora," Nature's Answer Web site, http://www.naturesanswer.com/articles/read_articles_searchresult.asp?id=33 (accessed April 30, 2007).

5. J. LaValle and W. G. Chambliss, "The Effect of Relora on Salivary Cortisol and DHEA Levels in Patients With Moderate to Severe Stress," Living Longer Clinic, Cincinnati, Ohio, 2001.

CHAPTER 10 • DIGESTIVE HEALTH

1. Fuller, *The Healing Power of Enzymes*, 118.

CHAPTER 11 • MIDLIFE PAINS—ARTHRITIS

1. J. M. Kremer et al., "Clinical Studies of n-3 Fatty Acids Supplementation in Patients With Rheumatoid Arthritis," *Rheumatic Disease Clinics* 17 (1992): 391–402, as quoted in Karin Granstrom Jordan, MD, "Osteoarthritis and Rheumatoid Arthritis," *Life Extension*, October 1999, http://www.lef.org/magazine/mag99/oct99-cover.html (accessed April 20, 2007).

2. A. Belluzi et al., "Effect of an Enteric-Coated Fish-Oil Preparation on Relapses in Crohn's Disease," *New England Journal of Medicine* 334, no. 24 (June 1996): 1557–1560.

3. J. M. Kremer et al., "Effects of High-Dose Fish Oil on Rheumatoid Arthritis After Stopping Nonsteroidal Anti-inflammatory Drugs; Clinical and Immune Correlates," *Arthritis and Rheumatism* 38, no. 8 (August 1995): 1107–1114; and C. S. Lau et al., "Effects of Fish Oil Supplementation on Non-Steroidal Anti-Inflammatory Drug Requirement in Patients With Mild Rheumatoid Arthritis—a Double-blind Placebo Controlled Study," *British Journal for Rheumatology* 32, no. 11 (November 1993): 982–989.

4. K. Engstrom et al., "Effect of Low-Dose Aspirin in Combination With Stable Fish Oil on Whole Blood Production of Eicosanoids," *Prostaglandins, Leukotrienes, and Essential Fatty Acids* 64, no. 6 (June 2001): 291–297.

CHAPTER 12 • CANCER

1. This checklist was given as a seminar handout by Hugh Shingleton, MD, national vice president for cancer detection and treatment, American Cancer Society.

2. L. S. Cook, M. L. Kamb, and N. S. Weiss, "Perineal Powder Exposure and the Risk of Ovarian Cancer," *American Journal of Epidemiology* 145, no. 5 (March 1997): 459–465, as reported by Reuters, quoted PersonalMD.com, "Ovarian Cancer Risk From Powdering," http://www.personalmd.com/news/a1997030701.shtml (accessed March 22, 2007).

CHAPTER 13 • DEPRESSION

1. J. F. Rosenbaumm et al., "The Antidepressant Potential of Oral S-Adenosyl-L-Methionine," *Acta Psychiatrica Scandinavia* 81, no. 5 (May 1990): 432–436.

2. K. Zmilacher, R. Bettegay, and M. Gastpar, "L-5-Hydroxytryptophan Alone and in Combination With a Peripheral Decarboxylase Inhibitor in the Treatment of Depression," *Neuropsychobiology* 20, no. 1 (1988): 28–35.

3. O. M. Wolkowitz, "Antidepressant and Cognition-Enhancing Effects of DHEA in Major Depression," *Annals of the New York Academy of Sciences* 774 (December 1995): 337–339.

CHAPTER 14 • HEALTH SCREENINGS FOR WOMEN

1. Taken from Saint Joseph Regional Medical Center's Health Library, "Ten Screening Tests Women Need," http://sjmed.netreturns .biz/HealthInfo/Story.aspx?StoryID=2417d7d6-4817-4d2f-b25b -9ffd311156d1 (accessed April 24, 2007).

CHAPTER 15 • PERIMENOPAUSE

1. John R. Lee with Virginia Hopkins, *What Your Doctor May Not Tell You About Menopause* (New York: Warner Books, 1996), 71.

2. John R. Lee, Jesse Hanley, and Virginia Hopkins, *What Your Doctor May Not Tell You About Premenopause* (New York: Warner Books, 1999), 60.

CHAPTER 16 • NEXT STOP: MENOPAUSE

1. S. Lieberman, "A Review of the Effectiveness of Cimicifuga Racemosa (Black Cohosh) for the Symptoms of Menopause," *Journal of Women's Health* 7, no. 5 (June 1998): 525–529; A. Petho, "Menopausal Complaints: Changeover of a Hormone Treatment to an Herbal Gynecological Remedy Practicable?" *Arztliche Prax Gynakol* 38 (1987): 1551–1553.

2. R. D. Gambrell, R. C. Maier, and B. I. Sanders, "Decreased Incidence of Breast Cancer in Postmenopausal Estrogen-Progesterone Users," *Obstetrics and Gynecology* 62 (1983): 435–443; John R. Lee, "Osteoporosis Reversal: The Role of Progesterone," *International Clinical Nutrition Review* 10, no. 3 (July 1990): 384–391; O. Picazo and A. Fernandez-Guasti, "Anti-Anxiety Effects of Progesterone and Some of Its Reduced Metabolites: An Evaluation Using the Burying Behavior Test," *Brain Research* 680 (May 1995): 135–141; and J. C. Prior, "Progesterone as a Bone Trophic Hormone," *Endocrine Reviews* 11, no. 2 (May 1990): 386–398.

CHAPTER 17 • BREAST HEALTH/BREAST DISEASE

1. L. D. Cowan et al., "Breast Cancer Incidence in Women With a History of Progesterone Deficiency," *American Journal of Epidemiology* 114, no. 2 (Aug 1981): 209–217.

2. J. M. Foidart et al., "Estradiol and Progesterone Regulate the Proliferation of Human Breast Epithelial Cells," *Fertility and Sterility* 69, no. 5 (May 1998): 963–969.

3. K. J. Chang et al., "Influences of Percutaneous Administration of Estradiol and Progesterone on Human Breast Epithelial Cell Cycle In Vivo," *Fertility and Sterility* 63, no. 4 (April 1995): 785–791.

4. R. K. Tiwari et al., "Selective Responsiveness of Human Breast Cancer Cells to Indole-3-Carbinol, a Chemopreventive Agent," *Journal of the National Cancer Institute* 86, no. 2 (January 1994): 126–131.

5. N. Pashby et al., "A Clinical Trial of Evening Primrose Oil in Mastalgia," *British Journal of Surgery* 68 (1981): 801–824.

6. P. R. Band et al., "Treatment of Benign Breast Disease With Vitamin A," *Preventative Medicine* 13, no. 5 (September 1984): 549–554.

CHAPTER 19 • GOTTA GO RIGHT NOW!—URINARY TRACT HEALTH

1. J. Avorn et al., "Reduction of Bacteriuria and Pyuria After Ingestion of Cranberry Juice," *Journal of the American Medical Association* 271, no. 10 (March 1994): 751–754.

CHAPTER 20 • MALE MENOPAUSE—ANDROPAUSE

1. Kimberly T. Brill et al., "Single and Combined Effects of Growth Hormone and Testosterone Administration on Measures of Body Composition, Physical Performance, Mood, Sexual Function, Bone Turnover, and Muscle in Healthy Older Men," *Journal of Clinical Endocrinology and Metabolism* 87, no. 12 (December 2002): 5649–5657.

2. K. Suzuki et al., "Synergistic Effects of Estrogen With Androgen on the Prostate—Effects of Estrogen on the Prostate of Androgen-Administered Rats and 5-Alpha-Reductase Activity," *The Prostate* 25, no. 4 (October 1994): 169–176.

3. A. Gray et al., "Age, Disease, and Changing Sex Hormone Levels in Middle-Aged Men: Results of the Massachusetts Male Aging Study," *Journal of Clinical Endocrinology and Metabolism* 73, no. 5 (November 1991): 1016–1025.

4. P. J. Pugh et al., "Testosterone: A Natural Tonic for the Failing Heart?" *QJM: Monthly Journal of the Association of Physicians* 93, no. 10 (October 2000): 689–694.

5. Eugene Shippen, MD, and William Fryer, *The Testosterone Syndrome* (New York: M. Evans and Company, 2001).

6. J. T. Kellis and L. E. Vickery, "Inhibition of Human Estrogen Synthetase (Aromatase) by Flavones," *Science* (September 1984): 1032–1034.

7. Gray et al., "Age, Disease, and Changing Sex Hormone Levels in Middle-aged Men."

8. Pugh et al., "Testosterone: A Natural Tonic for the Failing Heart?"

9. A. Elisabeth Hak et al., "Low Levels of Endogenous Androgens Increase the Risk of Atherosclerosis in Elderly Men: The Rotterdam Study," *Journal of Clinical Endocrinology and Metabolism* 87, no. 8 (August 2002): 3632–3639.

CHAPTER 21 • PROSTATE HEALTH AT FIFTY

1. "Saw Palmetto, African Prune and Stinging Nettle for Benign Prostatic Hyperplasia (BPH)," *Canadian Pharmaceuticals Journal* 130, no. 9 (1997): 37–44, 62.

2. M. Paubert-Braquet, "Effect of Serenoa Repens Extract (Permixon) on Estradiol/Testosterone-Induced Experimental Prostate Enlargement in the Rat," *Pharmacological Research* 34 (1996): 171–179.

CHAPTER 22 • YOUR EYESIGHT AND YOU

1. J. A. Mares-Perlman et al., "Vitamin Supplement Use and Incident Cataracts in a Population-Based Study," *Archives of Ophthalmology* 118, no. 11 (November 2000): 1556–1563.

2. R. Boniface and A. M. Robert, "Effect of Anthocyanins on Human Connective Tissue Metabolism in the Human," *Klinische Monatsblatter fur Augenheilkunde* 209, no. 6 (December 1996): 368–372.

3. J. T. Landrum et al., "A One Year Study of the Macular Pigment: The Effect of 140 Days of a Lutein Supplement," *Experimental Eye Research* 65, no. 1 (July 1997): 57–62.

4. M. Kuzniarz et al., "Use of Vitamin Supplements and Cataract: The Blue Mountains Eye Study," *American Journal of Ophthalmology* 132, no. 1 (July 2001): 19–26.

5. A. Wegener et al., "Experimental Evidence for Interactive Effects of Chronic UV Irradiation and Nutritional Deficiencies in the Lens," *Developments in Ophthalmology* 35 (2002): 113–124.

CHAPTER 23 • WIRED BUT TIRED—ADRENAL EXHAUSTION

1. B. Dubin, W. J. MacLennan, and J. C. Hamilton, "Adrenal Function and Ascorbic Acid Concentrations in Elderly Women," *Gerontology* 24, no. 6 (1978): 473–476.

2. J. R. Thomas et al., "Tyrosine Improves Working Memory in a Multitasking Environment," *Pharmacology, Biochemistry, and Behavior* 64, no. 3 (November 1999): 495–500.

CHAPTER 24 • STOP AND SMELL THE ROSES—AROMATHERAPY

1. Taken from Janet Maccaro, *Breaking the Grip of Dangerous Emotions* (Lake Mary, FL: Siloam, 2001), 80–81.

CHAPTER 27 • MAGNESIUM MATTERS

1. Leo Galland, MD, "When Stress Shatters, Magnesium Saves," *GreatLife*, October 1998, 36–37.

2. Michael Shechter et al., "Effects of Oral Magnesium Therapy on Exercise Tolerance, Exercise-Induced Chest Pain, and Quality of Life in Patients With Coronary Artery Disease," *American Journal of Cardiology* 91, no. 5 (March 2003): 517–521.

CHAPTER 28 • THE ACID TEST

1. Susan Lark, "Your Acid/Alkaline Balance," *The Women's Pharmacy* (Potomac, MD: Phillips Health LLC, 2003), 14–15.

CHAPTER 29 • DIABETES? HERE'S SWEET SUCCESS

1. "Effect of Lipoic Acid (Thioctic Acid) on Peripheral Nerve of Experimental Diabetic Neuropathy," *Diabetes und Stoffwechsel* 5, no. 3, Supplement (1996): 94–97.

2. C. M. Davis and J. B. Vincent, "Chromium Oligopeptide Activates Insulin Receptor Tyrosine Kinase Activity," *Biochemistry* 36, no. 15 (April 1997): 4382–4385.

3. D. Koutsikos, B. Agroyannis, and H. Tzanatos-Exarchou, "Biotin for Diabetic Peripheral Neuropathy," *Biomedicine and Pharmacotherapy* 44, no. 10 (1990): 511–514.

CHAPTER 30 • MIDLIFE IMMUNITY

1. H. E. Renis, "In Vitro Antiviral Activity of Calcium Elenolate," *Antimicrobial Agents and Chemotherapy* 9 (1969): 167–172. See also www.oliveleafextract.com.

2. K. Folkers and A. Wolaniuk, "Research on Coenzyme Q_{10} in Clinical Medicine and in Immunomodulation," *Drugs Under Experimental and Clinical Research* 11, no. 8 (1985): 539–545.

3. "Coenzyme Q_{10}." *Alternative Medicine Review* 3, no. 1 (February 1998): 58–61; F. Gazdik et al., "Decreased Levels of Coenzyme Q_{10} in Patients With Bronchial Asthma," *Allergy* 57, no. 9 (September 2002): 811–814; C. Q. Ye et al., "A Modified Determination of Coenzyme Q_{10} in Human Blood and CoQ_{10} Blood Levels in Diverse Patients With Allergies," *BioFactors* 1, no. 4 (December 1988): 303–306; F. L. Rosenfeldt et al., "Skeletal Myopathy Associated With Nucleoside Reverse Transcriptase Inhibitor Therapy: Potential Benefit of Coenzyme Q_{10} Therapy," *International Journal of STD and AIDS* 16, no. 12 (December 2005): 827–829.

4 T. H. Abdullah, D. V. Kirkpatrick, and J. Carter, "Enhancement of Natural Killer Cell Activity in AIDS With Garlic," *Deutsch Zeishrift fur Onkologie* 21 (1989): 52–53; see also P. P. Tadi et al., "Anti-Candidal and Anti-Cancerogenic Potentials for Garlic,"

International Clinical Nutrition Review 10, no. 4 (October 1990): 423–429.

5. J. Bernstein et al., "Depression of Lymphocyte Transformation Following Oral Glucose Ingestion," *American Journal of Clinical Nutrition* 30 (1977): 613.

6. R. W. Bartrop, "Depressed Lymphocyte Function After Bereavement," *Lancet* 1 (1977): 834–836.

7. J. Barone, J. R. Hebert, and M. M. Reddy, "Dietary Fat and Natural-Killer-Cell Activity," *American Journal of Clinical Nutrition* 50 (October 1989): 861–867.

CHAPTER 33 • SMILE! YOU'RE FIFTY—PERIODONTAL HEALTH

1. E. G. Wilkinson et al., "Bioenergetics in Clinical Medicine. II. Adjunctive Treatment With Coenzyme Q in Periodontal Therapy," *Research Communications in Chemical Pathology and Pharmacology* 12, no. 1 (September 1975): 111–123.

2. M. T. Khayyal, M. A. el-Ghazaly, and A. S. el-Khatib, "Mechanisms Involved in the Anti-Inflammatory Effect of Propolis Extract," *Drugs Under Experimental and Clinical Research* 19, no. 5 (1993): 197–203.

3. S. You, "Study on Feasibility of Chinese Green Tea Polyphenols (CTP) for Preventing Dental Caries," *Chinese Journal of Stomatalogy* 28, no. 4 (July 1993): 197–199, 254.

4. R. I. Vogel, "The Effect of Folic Acid on Gingival Health," *Journal of Periodontology* 47, no. 11 (1976): 667–668.

CHAPTER 34 • HEALTHY BRAIN, HEALTHY MIND

1. T. Cenacchi et al., "Cognitive Decline in the Elderly: A Double-Blind, Placebo-Controlled Multicenter Study on Efficacy of Phosphatidylserine Administration," *Aging* (Milano) 5, no. 2 (April 1993): 123–33.

2. Billie Jay Sahley and Katherine Birkner, *Heal With Amino Acids and Nutrients* (San Antonio, Tex.: Pain and Stress Publications, 2001); see also Billie Jay Sahley, *GABA: The Anxiety Amino Acid* (San Antonio, TX: Pain and Stress Publications, 2003). For more information, visit the Pain and Stress Center Web site at www .painstresscenter.com.

3. Billie Jay Sahley, *The Anxiety Epidemic*, 5th ed. (San Antonio, TX: Pain and Stress Publications, 2002).

4. A. Kobayashi et al., "Effects of L-Theanine on the Release of A-Brain Waves in Human Volunteers," *Nippon Noegikagaku Kaishi* 72 (1998): 153–157.

5. Kari Watson, "The Brain's Balancing Act," *Natural Health*, September/October 1998, 60–69.

APPENDIX • FIFTY WAYS TO EXTEND YOUR DAYS

1. N. T. Telang et al., "Inhibition of Proliferation and Modulation of Estradiol Metabolism: Novel Mechanisms for Breast Cancer Prevention by the Phytochemical Indole-3-Carbinol," *Proceedings of the Society for Experimental Biology and Medicine* 216 (November 1997): 246–252.

2. Zmilacher, "L-5-Hydroxytryptophan Alone and in Combination With a Peripheral Decarboxylase Inhibitor in the Treatment of Depression."

3. Kobayashi, "Effects of L-Theanine on the Release of A-Brain Waves in Human Volunteers."

4. E. M. Duker et al., "Effects of Extracts From Cimicifuga Racemosa on Gonadotropin Release in Menopausal Women and Ovariectomized Rats," *Planta Medica* 57, no. 5 (October 1991): 420–424.

5. T. E. McAlindon, M. P. LaValley, and D. T. Felson, "Efficacy of Glucosamine and Chondroitin for Treatment of Osteoarthritis," *Journal of the American Medical Association* 284, no. 10 (September

2000): 1241; see also V. R. Pipitone, "Chondroprotection with Chondroitin Sulfate," *Drugs Under Experimental and Clinical Research* 17, no. 1 (1991): 3–7.

6. O. Kucuk et al., "Lycopene Supplementation in Men With Prostate Cancer (PCa) Reduces Grade and Volume of Preneoplacia (PIN) and Tumor, Decreases Serum PSA and Modulates Biomarkers of Growth and Differentiation," Karmanos Cancer Institute, Wayne State University, Detroit, Michigan, 1999.

7. B. Andallu and B. Radhika, "Hypoglycemic, Diuretic and Hypocholesterolemic Effect of Winter Cherry (Withania Somnifera, Dunal) Root," *Indian Journal of Experimental Biology* 38, no. 6 (June 2000): 607–609.

8. E. Haak et al., "Effects of Alpha-Lipoic Acid on Microcirculation in Patients With Peripheral Diabetic Neuropathy," *Experimental and Clinical Endocrinology and Diabetes* 108, no. 3 (2000): 168–174.

9. N. Crespo et al., "Comparative Study of the Efficacy and Tolerability of Policosanol and Lovastatin in Patients With Hypercholesterolemia and Noninsulin Dependent Diabetes Mellitus," *International Journal of Clinical Pharmacology* Research 19, no. 4 (1999): 117–127.

BIBLIOGRAPHY, REFERENCES, AND SUGGESTED READING

Cooper, Kenneth H., MD, MPH. *Regaining the Power of Youth at Any Age.* Nashville: Thomas Nelson, 2005.

Fuller, DicQie, PhD, DSc. *The Healing Power of Enzymes.* New York: Forbes Inc., 1998.

Lark, Susan, MD. "Woman's Wellness Today." Healthy Directions, LLC.

Lee, John R., MD, with Virginia Hopkins, *What Your Doctor May Not Tell You About Menopause.* New York: Warner Books, 2004.

Life Extension Foundation. *Disease Prevention and Treatment Protocols,* 3rd expanded edition. Ft. Lauderdale, FL: Life Extension Media, 2000.

Maccaro, Janet C., PhD, CNC. *90-Day Immune System Makeover,* revised and updated ed. Lake Mary, FL: Siloam, 2006.

———. *Breaking the Grip of Dangerous Emotions.* Lake Mary, FL: Siloam, 2001.

———. *Natural Health Remedies: An A–Z Family Guide.* Lake Mary, FL: Siloam, 2003, 2006.

Northrup, Christiane, MD. *The Wisdom of Menopause.* New York: Bantam Books, 2001.

Page, Linda, PhD. *Healthy Healing,* 12th edition. Del Rey Oaks, CA: Healthy Healing Publications, 2004.

Sahley, Billie J. *The Anxiety Epidemic,* 5th edition. San Antonio, TX: Pain and Stress Publications, 2002.

OTHER BOOKS BY JANET MACCARO, PHD, CNC

Natural Health Remedies: An A–Z Family Guide

Breaking the Grip of Dangerous Emotions

90-Day Immune System Makeover

A Woman's Body Balanced By Nature

DR. JANET'S BALANCED BY NATURE FORMULAS

- Tranquility—for stress and anxiety

- Safe Passage—for perimenopausal and menopausal support

- Women's Balance Formula—progesterone cream

- Men's Balance Formula—pregnenolone and beta-sitosterol

- Skin Cream—for collagen and elastin

- SkinTastic—for body cleansing

- Beach Buffer—a natural exfoliator

- Coconut Dream—a rich body cream

For more information, visit Dr. Maccaro's Web site at www.DrJanetPhD .com.

Experience Better Health
in All Areas of Your Life Today!

We hope that you have discovered a new way to look at midlife in *Fabulous at 50*. Here are two more books by Janet Maccaro that will help you look and feel great in the years to come.

Natural Health Remedies—Revised
978-1-59185-897-3 / $17.99

Arm yourself with the health tips and tools you need to be renewed and restored to good health naturally!

A Woman's Body Balanced by Nature
978-1-59185-968-0 / $19.99

The manual for women's health, this book gives you the information you need for hormonal health, beauty, weight control, relationship issues, and *more!*

Visit your local bookstore today.

SILOAM
A STRANG COMPANY